现代汉语书面语学习手册

A Learners' Handbook of
Modern Chinese Written Expressions

冯禹 编著
By Yu Feng

The Chinese University Press

ISBN 962–201–868–8

THE CHINESE UNIVERSITY PRESS
The Chinese University of Hong Kong
Sha Tin, N.T., Hong Kong
Fax: +852 2603 6692
     +852 2603 7355
E-mail: cup@cuhk.edu.hk
Web-site: www.cuhk.edu.hk/cupress

Printed in Hong Kong

目 录
Contents

前 言
Preface

这本手册是为学习高级汉语(三年级及以上)的学生编写的。根据我们的教学经验，三年级的学生开始接触中文书报时会遇到很大的困难。这很自然，因为口语是任何一种语言的基础，所以一、二年级的汉语课，都是以口语为中心，课文以对话和口语化的小故事为主，很少涉及书面语。现在的课文是报纸上的新闻报道或杂志上的论文，大都是典型的现代汉语书面语，有许多特殊的表达方式、陌生的句型和词汇、更复杂的句子结构、大量的成语和缩略语等等。

This handbook is written for students of advanced Chinese (third year and up). According to our teaching experience, a student who has completed intermediate Chinese and is quite fluent in spoken Chinese will encounter tremendous difficulties in reading Chinese newspapers and journals when starting a course in advanced Chinese. Since the spoken language is always the basis of any language, the focus of our instruction at the beginner and intermediate levels has been on oral expression; the texts are either conversations or short stories narrated in the vernacular. In advanced Chinese, the news reports and articles in academic journals a student is assigned to read are written in a remarkably different way: They have special and more complicated sentence patterns, different vocabulary, more idioms, and frequent abbreviations.

什么是书面语？按照字面上的意思，书面语就是写出来的语言，口语是说出来的语言。一方面，口语是书面语的基础，先有口语，然后才有记录下来的书面语。事实上，大多数句型和词汇在日常会话和书写中都使用。另一方面，我们却又不能否认，口语和书面语有很多不同之处。有些说法主要是在口语中出现，现代汉语口语中有些词汇很难，甚至根本无法书写；另外一些说法则主要出现在书面，在日常会话中很不容易听到。

What is written language? According to the term itself, it denotes the expressions that are written in contrast to spoken language or the expressions as they are used in conversation. On one hand, spoken language is the basis of written language. A language is first spoken and only later recorded in the written form. Consequently, most expressions and idioms can be used in both writing and speech. On the other hand, however, one should not ignore the differences between them. Some expressions are most likely to appear in speech, and among them, some do not even have a written form, while others are most likely to appear in writing and are rarely heard in daily conversation.

　　书面语和口语的第一个差别在于，从功能上看，书面语是比较正式的语言，口语是比较随便的语言。如果在日常生活会话中使用书面语，有时会给人一种滑稽的感觉。同样的道理，如果在严肃的论文中使用非常口语化的说法，也会使人感到不伦不类。对于有些比较严肃的话题，即使是口说也要采取比较正式的说法。正因为如此，电台或者电视台在播放政治新闻和国际新闻的时候基本上采用和书面语相同或相近的词汇和句型。

The first difference between written and spoken expressions lies in their different functions: Written language is more formalized while spoken language tends to be informal. If one uses expressions specific to the written language in a conversational setting, this may even create a ridiculous effect. For the same reason, if one uses expressions that are only used in spoken language, the writing may sound similarly bizarre. However, for some specific formats, the usage of formal language patterns is necessary or appropriate to the discussion. This is the reason why broadcast or TV announcers use the same or similar patterns and vocabulary as written language when they announce political or international news.

　　书面语和口语的第二个差别在于，从来源上看，书面语保留着更多的古典的词语。很多古代的说法在现代汉语的口语中已经消失，但是书面语却照样使用。汉语书面语的虚词和成语，通常都是古代汉语遗留下来的痕迹。

The second difference between written and spoken expressions lies in their sources. In written language, classical words and phrases occur more frequently. Many ancient expressions have disappeared in modern spoken language, yet are still used in written expressions. The specialized function words and idioms of the written expressions are generally remnants of the classical Chinese style.

　　口语和书面语的上述两方面的区别，大概是中文、英文或者其他语言所共有的。例如英文的论文和法律文书倾向于使用比较古典的词汇和结构，有时夹杂着一些拉丁文或法文的短语，在日常口语对话中难以听到。但是，现代汉语书面语的运用范围更广泛，和日常生活密切相关。虽然现代汉语书面语同古代汉语有密切的关系，我们不应该把它看成一种缺乏生气的过时的语言。事实上，书面语是中国现代生活中的一个重要的部分，是报纸、书籍、文件的主导语言，至今仍看不出衰亡的迹象。甚至连公共场合的标识语，一般都使用和口语不同的有明显古典色彩的书面语。

The two differences between spoken language and written language can be observed in Chinese, English, and many other languages. Take for example, the academic treatises or legal documents in English are inclined to use classical expressions rarely heard in daily speech, such as Latin and French phrases. The special written expressions in modern Chinese have a wider application than their Western counterparts, and have a closer link to everyday life. In fact, written Chinese is a significant part of modern Chinese life, and is the dominant style of newspapers, books and documents. Nor do we see any sign of its impending demise. Even the most common warning signs seen in public areas often use the classical style.

汉语书面语和口语的一个独特的差别是，书面语可以把口语中的多音节词汇省略为单音节词汇，这可能和汉语语音的特性有关。每一个汉字是一个音节，并且具有特定的含义。由于同音字很多，所以在口语中为了避免误解，常常需要使用双音节或更多音节的词汇。但是汉字不是拼音文字，同音字的书写形式是不同的，阅读时不会发生误解。例如，"鲤"在说话的时候只能说鲤鱼，但是在文章中可以只使用一个鲤字。

A unique difference between written and spoken Chinese is that written expressions may abbreviate many multi-character words into single character words. This is probably related to the nature of the Chinese language. Every Chinese character is a single syllable, and denotes special meaning or meanings. Because many characters share a common pronunciation with others, oral expressions often need to use dual syllable or multi-syllable words to avoid misunderstanding. However, a character that shares a common pronunciation with other characters usually has a written form that clearly distinguishes it from the others. Therefore, when it is read, the chance of confusing it with another character is not likely. For example, to mention *li* (carp) orally, you have to say *liyu* (*yu* means fish) because *li* may also mean fox, plum, mile, etc. But when written, you may simply use the character *li* without *yu* to follow, and there will be no risk of misunderstanding because the radical, fish, is already a component of the character.

刚刚讨论的这个特点并不意味着书面语永远比口语简练。有时为了更精确地表达意思，书面语需要对于一些简单的词汇作修饰，把口语中最常用的一些单音节词汇变成双音节或多音节。例如"有"这个词，根据上下文的内容，书面语常常会采用"具有"、"拥有"、"享有"等更为确切的词汇。

Take note that this does not imply that written expression is always more concise than oral expression. Sometimes, in order to express one's meaning more precisely, a writer needs to modify some common words by adding one or more characters to them to create words with two or more syllables, which are used mainly for written expressions. For example, *you* — "to have" in the written language — will change due to different contexts into *juyou*, *yongyou*, and *xiangyou*. Although all of these words share the same common meaning of "to have," each has subtly different connotations in its usage.

为了更加简练和精确，书面语常常把口语中的比较短的几句话变成一句比较长的话，较多采用定语从句。这和西方语言比较接近，很可能受到了西方语言的影响。汉语书面语中的不少插入语，以及超长的句子结构，却常常是脱胎于西方语言，更确切地说，是翻译西方著作的一个副产品。

To make writing both concise and precise, a writer often tries to convert several short sentences into a single long sentence with relative clauses. This practice is similar to that of Romance and Germanic language families of the West, and may have actually been influenced by them. Some instances of parentheses and extremely long sentences in written Chinese are often taken directly from translation of Western languages.

一个非常有趣的现象是，在节奏和韵律方面，汉语书面语和口语常常有不同的要求。例如，书面语的单音节动词后面，常常需要连接单音节的动词宾语，而双音节动词后边，常常要求只能接双音节词，形成二字或四字格式。而口语常见的形式是单音节动词后连接双音节宾语，形成三字结构。书面语中广泛使用有古典影响的稳定的四字成语，口语中则广泛使用活泼幽默的三字俗语。

It is also interesting to note that the prosodic structures of written and spoken expressions have their own respective requirements. For example, in written expressions, certain verbs must be followed by double-character words while others require single-character words in order to achieve a phrase that is either of four characters or two characters in length. In contrast, a common pattern in spoken expressions is to follow a single syllable verb with a two-syllable object or a two-syllable verb followed by a single syllable object in order to create a three-character phrase. Written expressions frequently use four-character idioms, which have long-standing and unchanging classical definitions. This contrasts with oral expressions, which often prefer three-character idioms that are modern creations derived from vernacular style and societal humor.

同为书面语，我们可以看到许多不同的风格和形式。

Of course, different authors employ different styles and forms.

不同作品的"书面语化"的程度受到诸多因素的影响：其一，地区因素。一般来说，台湾和香港的作品的书面语化超过大陆，特别是古代汉语的词汇使用更多。其二，专业因素。历史学家的著作由于受到内容的影响，使用古汉语的频率非常高。而有些文学作品，特别是小说，常常是极为口语化的。其三，个人因素。有的作者至今还习惯使用半文半白的文体，也有些作者受西方语言影响非常明显，喜欢使用"欧化"句子，另外一些作者则几乎完全用"大白话"写作。

There are many factors that may influence the proclivity to use a formal, written style of language. The first is the regional origin of the text. Generally, the works by Taiwanese and Hong Kong authors often have a tendency to use a more classical style of Chinese. The second factor is professional requirements. The works of historians must use many ancient expressions due to their contents. The last factor is personal style. Today some authors still insist on the "half-classical" and "half-modern" style. Some are apparently influenced by Western languages and are fond of writing so-called "Europeanized sentences." Others, by contrast, like to write in an unadorned, plain spoken language-style.

现代汉语书面语可以按内容和文体分为以下几种类型：

The modern Chinese written language can be classified into the following sub-types according to their contents:

1. 新闻报导
   News reports
2. 论文
   Treatises
3. 广告与产品说明书
   Advertisements and product manuals
4. 其他应用文
   Other "applied" writings
5. 信函
   Correspondence
6. 文学作品
   Literature

上面所说的这几种文体中的书面语有许多共同之处，但又各有特色。论文因重视思维的严密和复杂，长句很多；新闻报导特别多地应用省略和缩略语；信函公文则有专门的格式，有些特别古雅；文学作品比较复杂，因为风格多样而很难总结出典型性。有些文学作品非常口语化，甚至使用许多通俗口语的说法，直接记录未经修饰的地方话；也有一些文学作品半文半白，采用很多古典成语和其他描写手法。

Although the sub-types listed above have many common aspects, each has its own distinctive features. To emphasize the accurateness and complexity of logic, academic treatises are often characterized by long and complex sentences; in news reports, there are more ellipses and abbreviations; correspondence and documents have fixed forms, some of which are extremely formalized or even antiquated. Although literature (fiction, dramas, and poems) sometimes uses written language too, they have too many different styles and are thus atypical. Some fiction is colloquial to the point of imitating, without any refinement, people's utterances in their nearly unintelligible local dialects, while others are semi-classical and infused with a surfeit of old-fashioned idioms and expressions.

高级现代汉语的学习者是否应当比较系统地掌握书面语的知识？我们的答案是肯定的。这些学生学习汉语的目的，无论是对中国或东亚的某一方面作专门研究，还是准备去中国学习和工作，都应该具备阅读中文报刊、研究论文、信函文件等"应用文"的初步技能。不懂书面语，就不能真正了解中国社会，甚至难以在中国生存。上面已经提到，书面语是比较正式的语言，而能否在比较正式的场合理解并使用同日常生活会话有所区别的语言，是衡量学生水平的重要标志，也是目前一些高级中文考试的重要内容。

Should the advanced student of Chinese systematically learn the written language? Our answer is yes. Each student has a different reason for learning Chinese. Some will use the Chinese language as a tool to study specific aspects of China or other parts of East Asia; others are preparing to visit or live in China. No matter what reason students may have, they still need the basic ability to read Chinese newspapers, magazines, academic treatises, letters, notices, documents and other "applied writings." Otherwise, they will not be able to understand Chinese society, and will even find it difficult to survive in China. As described above, the written language is relatively formal. Whether you are able to understand and use formal, written Chinese is the criterion to judge the level of a student. Unsurprisingly, written expressions constitute a significant part of advanced Chinese tests.

一般地说，我们的目标是让学生看懂书面语，而不是让他们熟练地用书面语写作。然而，我们相信，做一些简单的书面语和口语的转换练习，包括从口语到书面语的转换，可能是提高阅读理解书面语的能力的好方法。何况，学生们也应当有用中文写信或写作表达自己的观点的短文的能力。

Overall, our goal is to help students understand written Chinese, not to make them experts in composition. We believe mutual conversion exercises between the spoken and written style is an effective way of improving students' ability in reading comprehension. Additionally, students should have the skills to write letters and express their opinions in short essays.

书面语的内容非常广泛，与口语的分界也不是非常清楚。本书的目的并非对现代汉语的书面语作学术研究。我们试图用最简明和最实用的方式向学生介绍最常见的现代汉语书面语惯用法。它的重点是论文、新闻报导和信函公文，因为学生更需要读这些文章，而且其表达方式相对说来比较有限，不像文学作品那样变化多端，漫无边际。虽然"手册"应该比较完备，但对于生僻罕见的书面语，一般不收入。对于收入的条目，尽可能分门别类，以使学生的认识更加系统化，也便于比较和记忆。

We are aware that the contents of modern written Chinese language is quite broad and there is no clear distinction between written and spoken expressions. The purpose of this handbook, then, is to serve neither as an encyclopedia of written expressions nor a scholarly research of their grammatical structure. Instead, we attempt to provide students with the most important written expressions and idioms in modern Chinese in a way that is both concise and practical. Although a handbook attempts to be as comprehensive as possible, we are not hesitant to exclude some seldom-used expressions and idioms. We try to classify the expressions and idioms in order to aid the student to learn more systematically and ease to comparison and memorization.

本手册分为两大部分。第一部分共十章，通论书面语的共同特征，包括语法、句法、词汇等。除了解释意义和用法，还提供例句。第二部分共六章，通过典型文例分论各种类型和体裁的特异之处，并附有专门词汇和短语等。本手册另附练习，以帮助学生巩固学到的知识。为了帮助学生更准确地理解，全书采用汉英对照的形式。

This handbook consists of two parts. There are twelve chapters in the first part, which deal with common knowledge of written expressions such as grammar, syntax, and vocabulary. Besides explaining the patterns, phrases, and words and introducing their usage, we also provide the readers with various sample sentences. The second part contains six chapters. Through typical examples, we explain the distinctive features of various sub-styles of written expressions with some special lexicons and idioms. An "Exercise" section is included at the end of this handbook to help students reinforce what they have just learned. Based on the assumption that students using this book have not fully mastered the Chinese language, this handbook is bilingual.

本手册作为哈佛大学东亚系中文部的一个研究项目，是在何宝璋主任的主持下，从一九九六年开始，由冯禹在李卉老师的指导下执笔编写。在编写过程中，先后得到李金玉、胡文泽、黄伟嘉等老师以及马修凡先生、芮尼克先生和珍德女士的协助，并曾在课堂教学中部分试用。本书的大部分例句是编者模仿中国报纸、政论文或学术论文的风格而撰写的，也参考了部分报纸和学术著作，谨在此致谢。

The writing of this handbook began in 1996 as a project of the Harvard Chinese Language Program planned and supervised by the program director, Dr. Baozhang He. In writing this book Yu Feng has been under the guidance of Huei Li Chang, and received help from Jinyu Li, Wenze Hu, Weijia Huang, Matthew Fragleigh, Nicholas Reisdorff and Tara Zend. Parts of this handbook have been tried in our Advanced Chinese classes. Most of the examples in this handbook, mirroring language used in Chinese newspapers, political or academic articles, are written by the author, who wishes to acknowledge references to newspapers and some academic works.

第 一 章 • 名 词
Chapter 1 • Nouns

书面语的名词常常省略，特别是专有名词，省略更为普遍。

In writing, nouns are often abbreviated, especially for proper nouns.

1.1 国名地名的缩略 (Abbreviation of Places)

1.1.1 取第一字 (using the first character)

美(国)	United States
日(本)	Japan
德(国)	Germany
法(国)	France
俄(罗斯)	Russia
西(班牙)	Spain
韩(国)	(South) Korea
朝(鲜)	(North) Korea
泰(国)	Thailand
马(来西亚)	Malaysia
新(加坡)	Singapore
埃(及)	Egypt
黑(龙江)	Heilongjiang (a province of China)

1.1.2 取第二字 (using the second character)

(北)京	Beijing

(天)津　　Tianjin

(香)港　　Hong Kong

(四)川　　Sichuan

1.1.3　取两字或两字以上 (using two or more characters)

印(度)尼(西亚)　　　　　Indonesia

阿(拉伯)联(合)酋(长国)　the United Arab Emirates

1.1.4　变换说法 (using different names)

沪(上海)　　Hu = Shanghai

鲁(山东)　　Lu = Shandong

粤(广东)　　Yue = Guangdong

晋(山西)　　Jin = Shanxi

豫(河南)　　Yu = Henan

冀(河北)　　Ji = Hebei

皖(安徽)　　Wan = Anhui

赣(江西)　　Gan = Jiangxi

湘(湖南)　　Xiang = Hunan

闽(福建)　　Mi = Fujian

黔(贵州)　　Qian = Guizhou

1.2　机构名称的缩略 (Abbreviation of Institutions and Organizations)

1.2.1　大 = 大会/大学

联大　联合国代表大会　　UN Assembly

人大　人民代表大会　　　People's Congress
　　　人民大学　　　　　The People's University of China

北大　北京大学　　　　　Peking University

1.2.2 委 = 委员会/委员

常委	常务委员会	standing committee
	常务委员	member of standing committee
地委	地区委员会	regional committee
体委	体育运动委员会	sport committee

1.2.3 联 = 联合会

| 妇联 | 妇女联合会 | Women's Federation |
| 青联 | 青年联合会 | Youth Federation |

1.2.4 协 = 协会

作协	作家协会	Authors' Association
记协	记者协会	Reporters' Association
足协	足球协会	Soccer Association

1.2.5 中 = 中央/中国

中纪委	中央纪律检查委员会	Central Commission of Discipline Inspection
中直	中央直属	Departments directly under the Central Authority
中船	中国船舶工业总公司	China Ship Building Company

1.2.6 办 = 办公室/办公厅

| 邓办 | 邓小平办公室 | The Secretariat Office of Deng Xiaoping |
| 侨办 | 侨务办公室 | Office of Overseas Chinese Affairs |

1.2.7 其他常见机构的省略 (other frequently seen abbreviations of institutes)

安理会	联合国安全理事会	UN Security Council
北约	北大西洋公约组织	NATO
东盟	东南亚国家联盟	ASEAN

居委会	居民委员会	neighborhood commission
国府	国民政府	R.O.C. government

1.3　事件/运动的缩略 (Abbreviation of Events, Movements, etc.)

1.3.1　运 = 运动/运动会 (movement/sport games)

工运	工人运动	workers movement
共运	共产主义运动	Communist Movement
奥运	奥林匹克运动会	Olympic Games
亚运	亚洲运动会	Asian Games

1.3.2　其他 (other abbreviations of frequently mentioned events and movements)

文革	文化大革命	Cultural Revolution
越战	越南战争	Vietnam War
七五	第七个五年计划	The Seventh Five-Year Plan
九大	第九次代表大会	The Ninth Congress
三中全会	中央委员会第三次全体会议	The Third Plenary Session of Central Committee
广交会	广州进出口商品交易会	Guangzhou Export Commodities Fair
严打	严厉打击犯罪活动	severe punishment of the criminals

1.4　其他 (Other Frequently Used Abbreviations)

高干	高级干部	high-ranking cadres
归侨	归国华侨	returned overseas Chinese
基建	基本建设	infrastructure construction
城建	城市建设	urban construction

地铁	地下铁路	subway
毛选	毛泽东选集	Selected Works of Chairman Mao

1.5 书面语常见但口语罕用的一部分名词 (Some General Nouns Frequently Used in Written Expressions but Rarely Used in Oral Expressions)

败笔	a faulty part in a good work	陋俗	undesirable custom
抱负	aspiration; ambition	路人	passerby
差异	difference	论断	thesis
常态	normality	论据	arguments
初衷	original intention	莽原	wilderness
歹徒	evildoer	梦幻	illusion
典范	model	梦呓	rigmarole
反响	reaction	迷途	wrong path
风波	disturbance	面目	appearance
风云	precarious situation	名次	position in a name list
光阴	time	谬误	falsehood
花絮	tidbits (of news)	畔	side, shore
基调	key note	瓶颈	bottle neck
迹象	sign	破绽	flaw
进程	process	区域	area, region
绝境	impasse	使命	mission
抉择	choice	仕途	official career
礼遇	courteous reception	事宜	matters, affairs
利弊	advantage and disadvantage	损益	increase and decrease
粮秣	rations and fodder	铁窗	prison
劣迹	misdeed	同窗	classmate
流言	rumor	同僚	colleague

途径	way, channel	效能	efficacy
微词	veiled criticism	预兆	presage, sign
闲暇	leisure	阅历	experience
笑柄	laughingstock	卓见	excellent vision

第 二 章 · 代 词
Chapter 2 • Pronouns

2.1 代词的修饰 (Modifier to Pronouns)

从语法上看，口语中代词前不可加定语，但书面语的代词前可以有定语，特别是文学描述的代词前可以有较长的定语。这一规则主要适用于单数人称代词我、你、他。

According to the grammar of spoken Chinese, modifiers should not be used before a pronoun. But in written Chinese, especially in literature, long modifiers can be placed before a pronoun. However, this rule is applied to single personal pronouns only.

> 平素很少喝茶的我也为当地的别具一格的茶道所吸引。
> Even I who seldom drink tea was still attracted by the distinctive tea ceremony of that region.

> 公司经理的一席话深深地打动了刚刚大学毕业的他。
> The speech of the executive of the company deeply moved him who had just graduated from college.

2.2 第一人称 (First Person)

2.2.1 我

在口语中，"我"只代表我自己，但是在书面语中，"我"常常可以表示"我们的"，甚至表示"我们国家"，"我国政府"等。

In oral expressions, the difference between *wo* and *women* is clear. But in written expressions, *wo* can be used to indicate "our" or even "our country" and "our government," etc.

> 我严正警告日本政府，违背两国间的协议将引起严重后果。
> <u>Our</u> government gave a stern warning to the Japanese government, stating that the transgression of the bilateral agreement would have serious consequences.

我校派出代表团赴南非访问。
Our university sent a delegation to visit South Africa.

敌机两架侵入我海南岛上空。
Two enemy airplanes intruded the territorial air space of (our) Hainan Island.

2.2.2 吾人 = 我们 (we, us)

这个说法在二、三十年代较为流行，现在大陆已经不用，台湾还有人使用。

Although quite popular in 1920s and 1930s, it is now obsolete in the mainland though still in use in Taiwan.

关于能源的合理利用，吾人前文已有详述。
As for the reasonable utility of resources, we have already detailed it in the previous chapters.

2.2.3 本 = 我的/我们的 (my/our)

因使用不当造成的损失，本公司概不负责。
Our company will not be responsible for any loss caused by improper usage.

本书主要讨论宋明儒学与佛教的关系问题。
The relationship between Song-Ming Neo-Confucianism and Buddhism is the main topic of our book.

2.2.4 敝 (modest expression of "our"/"my")

对于这次事故，敝公司将本着实事求是的精神加以调查。
For this accident, our company will undertake an investigation with the spirit of seeking truth from facts.

2.2.5 鄙人 (modest expression of "I"/"me," literally meaning "the humble")

鄙人愿为此承担一切责任。
I would like to take full responsibility for this.

2.2.6 拙 (modest expression of "my," literally meaning "the stupid")

拙著   my writing

拙荆   my wife

2.2.7 寒舍 (modest expression of "my home," literally meaning "the cold dorm")

请光临寒舍一叙。
Please come to my home to have a talk.

2.3 第二人称 (Second Person)

2.3.1 贵 (respectful expression of "your")

望贵校予以协助。
We wish for <u>your esteemed</u> institution to assist [us].

2.4 第三人称 (Third Person)

2.4.1 之

第三人称代词，可以代人、物或抽象的概念。通常见于成语中。

Pronoun for third person. It may represent people, things, or abstract concepts. Mainly used in idioms.

听之任之   let <u>something</u> go unchecked

等闲视之   regard <u>it</u> as unimportant

受之有愧   to feel shame if [I] accept <u>it</u> (an honor, a position, a gift, etc.) [because I do not deserve it]

2.4.2 其 (its, it, him, his, her, them, their)

作宾语或用作物主代词，不能用作主语。

Used as object or possessive pronoun. Cannot be used as subject.

大约在公元前六世纪中叶，《诗经》即已编订成书，而其具体作品的产生可以追溯到公元前十一世纪。
The *Book of Odes* was compiled as early as the mid-sixth century B.C., and the composition of the poems collected in <u>it</u> can be traced back to the eleventh century B.C.

总统再三强调把经济的发展放在首位，其目的是改变人们认为他不懂经济的印象。

The president repeatedly stressed giving priority to economic development. <u>His</u> goal is to change the impression that his knowledge of the economy is poor.

虽然很多人买了电脑，但对其功能却不甚了解。

Although many people have bought a computer, they often do not quite understand all of <u>its</u> various functions.

鉴于他的恶劣表现，公司领导决定立即将其开除。

In light of his irresponsible conduct, the company leaders decided to immediately fire <u>him</u>.

2.5 指示代词 (Demonstrative Pronouns)

2.5.1 该 (that)

表示"那个"，如"该国"、"该党"、"该生"(那个学生)、"该地"等等。

Meaning "that" such as "that country", "that party", "that student", "that place", etc.

该党领导人的讲话引起公众的普遍不满。

The speech delivered by the leader of <u>that</u> party upset the people.

2.5.2 此 (this)

此书在国内外多次获奖。

<u>This</u> book has repeatedly won awards both in China and abroad.

我们对此深表遗憾。

We feel very sorry for <u>this</u>.

2.6 不定代词 (Indefinite Pronoun)

2.6.1 某 (certain, some)

可放在名词前。

It can be placed before a noun.

某公司的一名司机目睹了这起事故。

A driver of a <u>certain</u> company witnessed this mishap.

这种造型独特的产品受到了某些消费者的欢迎。

With its unique shape, this product is welcomed by <u>some</u> consumers.

也可放在姓氏后面，通常是在不便说出姓名的情况下使用。在旧式书信中，可用来指代自己。

It can also be placed after a surname. It is used when for some reason the writer does not want to mention the given name. In old-style correspondence, the writer would sometimes use this technique to refer to himself.

北京市民杨某因吸毒和贩卖毒品被判处无期徒刑。

Yang, a native of Beijing, was sentenced to life imprisonment because of drug abuse and trafficking.

阁下大恩大德，王某感激不尽。

I feel very grateful and am obliged for your gracious benevolence and favor.

第 三 章 · 动 词
Chapter 3 · Verbs

汉语书面语同口语在动词方面的差别明显超过名词的差别。有许多动词是书面语专有的。与动词相关的语法和句法也有所不同。

The difference between written and oral expressions of verbs is greater than that of nouns. Many verbs are used in written expressions only. There are also grammatical and syntactical differences relating to verbs.

3.1 联系动词 (Link Verbs)

口语中的联系动词只有"是"，而书面语除了"是"以外，还常用以下联系动词：

In oral expressions, *shi* is the only link verb. In written expressions, there are the followings besides *shi*:

3.1.1 为

通常用于过去的情况。没有否定形式。

Often used for past situation. No negative form.

> 张志刚原为北京自行车厂工人。
> Zhang Zhigang used to be a worker in the Beijing Bicycle Factory.

3.1.2 乃

可以单独使用，也可以与"是"联用，语气较强。没有否定形式。

Can be used independently or together with *shi*. Often used for emphasis. No negative form.

> 掌握敌情乃(是)战争胜利之关键。
> Knowing the enemy well is the key to victory.

龙井乃绿茶之极品。
Longjing is the apex of green teas.

3.1.3 系

没有否定形式。

No negative form.

死者生前系北京友谊出租汽车有限公司司机。
The dead man was a driver of Beijing Friendship Taxi Inc.

说中国有扩张野心纯系谎言。
It is an unequivocal lie to assert that China has expansion ambitions.

3.2 助动词 (Helping Verbs)

书面语助动词同口语的区别比较明显。有一些口语中常用的双音节助动词在书面语中被简化为单音节。

For helping verbs, the differences between written and spoken expressions are quite obvious. A number of two-syllable helping verbs in spoken expressions are often simplified into single-syllable ones.

3.2.1 可 = 可以 (may, can)

这座体育场可容纳上万名观众。
This stadium <u>can</u> seat over ten thousand spectators.

3.2.2 应 = 应该 (should, ought to)

这封读者来信不应发表。
This reader's letter <u>should</u> not be published.

3.2.3 当 = 应当 (should, ought to)

攻占此城后你部当立即向西推进。
Immediately after occupying this city, your unit should advance westward.

3.2.4 须 = 必须 (must, have to)

退换商品须持发票及本人证件。
In order to return an item, you must present the original receipt and your identity card.

3.2.5 不得 = 不能 (may not)

注意：这里的"得"念 dé，不要与口语的"得"混淆。

Note: Do not confuse this *dé* with the oral expression *děi*.

> 未经许可，不得入内。
> No entrance without permission.

3.2.6 将 (will, shall)

> 江泽民主席将出访日本。
> President Jiang Zemin will visit Japan.

3.3 "进行"/"举行"/"实行" + 动词宾语 (*Jinxing/Juxing/Shixing* + Verbal Object)

这种结构在口语中也有，但书面语更为常见。注意：在上述动词后的动词宾语应该是双音节词，常见的是两个字或者四个字的。另外，动词宾语不能再有自己的宾语。然而，可以用"就"或者"对"引导出动作的对象。

This structure can be found in both oral and written expressions but more often in the latter. Note: First, the verbal object should be of even number, usually two or four characters; second, the verbal object cannot have its own object. However, you may use *jiu* or *dui* to introduce an object.

3.3.1 进行 (undergo)

> 当局许诺对事件进行重新调查。
> The authorities promised to re-investigate the incident.

3.3.2 举行 (hold)

> 中美两国领导人举行了将近两个小时的会谈。
> The leaders of China and the United States held a discussion for nearly two hours.

3.3.3 实行 (perform)

> 中国人民银行决定对外汇买卖实行控制。
> The People's Bank of China decided to enact measures to control the exchange of foreign currencies.

3.4 不及物动词作及物动词用 (Conversion of Intransitive Verb into Transitive Verb)

在书面语中，特别是在新闻报道和文学描述中，不及物动词作及物动词使用的情况较口语普遍。

In written expressions, the conversion of an intransitive verb into a transitive verb is more common than in oral expressions.

外商满意莱州税务官。(外商对莱州税务官表示满意。)
Foreign businessmen are satisfied with the tax collectors of Lai Zhou.

国务院出台有关政策。(国务院有关政策出台。)
The State Council issued related policies.

中美谈判知识产权。(中美两国就知识产权问题进行谈判。)
China and the United States held a discussion on intellectual property rights.

服务社会。(为社会服务。)
To serve society.

八十年代初，可口可乐登陆中国。(……在中国登陆。)
In the early 1980s, Coca-Cola made its first appearance in mainland China.

注意：这是一些有争议的语言现象，不宜效法。

Note: These conversions are controversial and not recommended for use by students.

3.5 被动结构 (Passive Voice)

3.5.1 为

书面语常常用"为"来代替"被"。

Bei is often replaced with *wei* in written expressions.

他的著作深为港台读者喜爱。
His works are greatly appreciated by readers in Hong Kong and Taiwan.

这个以前为人们鄙视的行业现在成为求职者竞争的热门。
This profession, of little interest to most people in the past, has now become a target of intense competition by job hunters.

3.5.2 隐藏被动结构 (hidden passive voice)

明显地有被动的意思但是却不用"被"或者相似的介词。在新闻报道等书面语中极为常见。有时，不仅是可以隐藏，而且是应当甚至必须隐藏。下面是一些比较典型的要求省略"被"的例句：

Some sentences that use the passive voice can hide *bei* or other similar prepositions. This is quite often the case in news reports and other sub-styles of written expressions. Sometimes, to hide *bei* is not only possible but necessary. The following are typical examples:

大批物资运往灾区。
A great amount of goods have been transported to the disaster area.

违者罚款。
Violators will be fined.

3.6 "将"代替"把" (*Jiang* in Place of *Ba*)

新建的铁路将落后的内地同发达的沿海地区连接起来了。
The newly constructed railroad connects the underdeveloped inland regions with the highly developed coast regions.

校方决定将这名屡教不改的学生开除。
The school principal decided to dismiss the student who persisted in his deliquency despite repeated warnings.

美国一直将中美洲视为自己的后院。
The United States has always regarded Central America as its backyard.

由于经费困难，中国社会科学院不得不将一些同国家利益无关的研究项目取消。
Due to a paucity of funds, the Chinese Academy of Social Sciences has had to withdraw from several research projects that are not pertinent to the national interests.

3.7 书面语动词表 (A List of Verbs of Written Expression)

此表罗列的是一些常用的书面语动词，或者同口语表达相异，或者没有相应的口语词汇。

Listed here are verbs frequently seen in written expressions which are either different from oral expressions or have no equivalent in oral expressions.

败北	suffer defeat	篡改	distort
褒贬	appraise	存	have
背弃	abandon (one's original stand or promise)	存有	have
		磋商	discuss
贬低	depreciate	导致	lead to (a consequence)
表白	vindicate	登载	publish (in a newspaper or magazine)
表彰	commend		
濒临	be on verge of	抵（达）	arrive
剥夺	deprive	抵制	boycott
驳斥	refute	颠覆	subvert, overturn
部署	dispose, deploy	定夺	make a final decision
参照	refer to	动容	be visibly moved
策划	plan, plot	动用	put to use
阐发	elucidate	洞察	see clearly
阐明	clarify	敦促	urge, press
倡导	initiate, propose	防范	be on guard
陈述	to state	放任	not interfere, let things drift
承	receive	诽谤	slander
乘（车等）	take (vehicle)	奉献	offer a tribute
惩处	penalize	服	take (medicine), serve (a sentence), be on (military service)
持	hold		
崇尚	uphold		
重申	reiterate (an opinion, policy, etc.)	伏法	be executed
		赴	leave for
辞行	say goodbye to	告终	come to an end
从略	be omitted	贯彻	implement
从事	be engaged in	归咎	impute to
促成	facilitate	规劝	admonish

轰动	cause a sensation	罗列	enumerate, list
呼吁	call on	罗织	frame up
挥霍	spend freely	落实	carry out
回顾	review	蒙	receive
鉴别	distinguish	藐视	despise, look down upon
较量	have a contest	觅	look for
解体	disintegrate	模拟	imitate
介入	intervene	抹杀	write off
借故	find an excuse	默哀	stand in silent tribute
借鉴	use for reference	默许	tacitly consent to
借重	rely on（support）	目睹	witness
就范	（force someone to）submit, give in	排斥	exclude
就绪	be ready	排解	mediate
具	have	聘请	invite（someone to a job）
具有	have	平息	calm down
开拓	open up	起草	to draft
凯旋	triumphantly return	企图	attempt
苛求	excessively demand	迁就	yield to
窥测	spy out	取缔	ban, suppress
离任	leave one's post (especially for ambassador)	权衡	weigh（the advantage and disadvantage of an action）
理应	ought to, should	热衷	hanker after
立足	base oneself upon	荣获	have the honor to win
列举	enumerate, list	容纳	hold, have a capacity
领会	understand, comprehend	润色	polish（an article）
领略	have a taste of	散布	spread
浏览	browse	商榷	discuss
履行	perform, fulfill	申辩	defend

深化	deepen	效尤	knowingly follow the example of a wrong doer
审议	deliberate		
声讨	denounce	卸任	be relieved of one's office
声援	express support	拥有	possess
实施	put into effect	遇难	die accidentally or be murdered
试图	attempt	曰	say
伺机	wait for one's chance	越轨	transgress
探索	research	赞同	agree
探究	research	臧否	pass judgment on
陶醉	be intoxicated	责成	instruct (somebody to do something)
誊写	transcribe		
停滞	stagnate	憎恶	detest
通晓	know well (certain knowledge)	瞻仰	look at with reverence
推敲	deliberate	展望	look into the future
脱稿	complete (a writing)	肇事	cause trouble
脱险	escape a danger	甄别	examine and distinguish
唾弃	cast aside, spurn	斟酌	consider, deliberate
挽留	urge someone to stay	争执	argue, conflict
婉拒	politely refuse	正告	warn sternly
亡故	die	质疑	call in question
忘却	forget	致辞	make a speech
违章	break rules	追随	follow somebody closely
问罪	condemn	追溯	trace back to
诬蔑	slander, vilify	赘述	describe redundantly
无补	have no help	准予	grant
享年	die at the age of	着手	set about
消亡	die out		

第四章・连接词语
Chapter 4 • Conjunctions

4.1 并列 (Juxtaposition)

4.1.1 与 = 和 (and/with)

主要用在名词或名词从句之间。

Used between nouns and between phrases.

> 李白与杜甫是唐代最伟大的诗人。
> Li Bai <u>and</u> Du Fu were the two greatest poets of the Tang dynasty.

> 他的论点与钱穆先生所说的大同小异。
> The difference between his arguments <u>and</u> what Mr. Qian Mu said are minor.

4.1.2 同 = 和 (and/with)

用在名词或名词从句之间，常常有比较的意思。

Used between nouns, often indicating comparison.

> 中国文化同印度文化比较，有着根本的差别。
> In comparing Chinese <u>and</u> Indian culture, one finds fundamental differences.

> 在人权问题上，中国同美国有很大的分歧。
> China <u>and</u> the United States have great differences in approach to human rights.

4.1.3 而 (yet/and)

用在两个形容词之间。

Used between adjectives.

> 少而精。
> Lesser in quantity <u>yet</u> better in quality.

山西阳泉出产的煤炭轻而易燃。

The coal mined from Yangquan in Shanxi Province is both light in weight <u>and</u> easy to burn.

* 有转折意义的"而"，见 4.4.4。

For *er* which has transitional meaning, see 4.4.4.

4.1.4　则 (while/whereas)

放在下半句的主语之后，表示"与此同时"，有比较和转折的意思。

Placed after the subjective of the second clause to indicate comparison and/or transition.

> 中国是一个有五千年文明史的国家，美国则是一个只有三百年历史的新兴国家。
> China is a nation with a history of civilization over 5,000 years <u>whereas</u> the United States is a "young" country with only 300 years of history.

> 欣赏工业文明的人常歌颂近代史为人类进步的高峰；厌恶者则引人类日益陷于物质欲望之中而莫能自拔为深忧。
> <u>While</u> those who appreciate industrial civilization extol modern history as the pinnacle of human progress, those who disagree are extremely concerned over that human kind is irretrievably mired in material desires.

* "则"的其他用法见 4.6.5。

For other usage of *ze*, see 4.6.5.

4.1.5　且 (and)

是"而且"的省略，只用于书面语。

As abbreviation of *erqie*, used in written language only.

> 这种新药疗效甚佳，且无明显的副作用。
> This new medicine is extremely effective, <u>and</u> it does not have any apparent side-effects.

4.1.6　并 (and)

在主语不变的情况下引导并列句。

Used in the beginning of another sentence with the same subject as the previous sentence.

美国总统将同中国主席举行会谈，并将访问上海、杭州等城市。

The President of the United States will meet with the President of China, <u>and</u> then will visit Shanghai, Hangzhou, and other cities.

4.1.7 （以）及 (as well as)

与"和"相似，但是通常在"及"之前是最重要的东西，在"及"之后是次重要的东西。

Similar to *he*, but generally what is placed before *ji* is more important than what is placed after it.

> 这位中医擅长治疗心脏病及高血压。
> This doctor of Chinese medicine is talented at treating heart diseases <u>as well as</u> hypertension.

> 他对中国、日本以及其他东亚各国的事务，都有深刻的了解。
> He has a deep understanding of the affairs of China and Japan, <u>as well as</u> other Asian countries.

4.2 假设 (Assumption)

4.2.1 倘若（倘）……就（则）(if ... will/would)

等于口语中的"要是……就"，多用在比较严肃的背景下。

Similar to the spoken expression "*yaoshi ... jiu,*" but mainly used in serious situations.

> 倘若稍有疏忽，就会导致重大的事故。
> Were there even a slight oversight, a serious accident <u>will</u> take place.

4.2.2 否则 = 要是不这样 (otherwise)

用在下半句的开始，后面可以接"将"。上半句常常有"必须"、"应该"等语。

Used at the beginning of the second clause, and may be followed by *jiang*. As coordination, *bixu* or *yinggai* is often used in the first clause.

> 政府必须有效地控制通货膨胀，否则将有可能发生大规模的社会动乱。
> The government must effectively control inflation. <u>Otherwise</u>, large-scale social chaos will ensue.

4.2.3 如若不然 = 要是不这样 (otherwise)

与"否则"相同。

The usage is the same as *fouze.*

> 经济学家应该注意新技术对工商业的影响，如若不然，经济预测是不可能准确的。
> Economists should pay attention to the impact of new technology on business, <u>otherwise</u> their economic predictions may not be accurate.

4.2.4 若 (if)

在古汉语中，常常单独使用，意思和"如果"差不多；而在现代汉语书面语中，常常与"能"、"要"、"想"等词连用。

In classical Chinese, *ruo* is frequently used and is similar to *ruguo* in modern Chinese. In modern Chinese written expressions, *ruo* is often used together with *neng, yao, xiang,* etc.

> 若能进一步发挥乡镇企业的潜力，中国的经济在十年中将会有更快的发展。
> <u>If</u> the potential of township enterprises <u>can</u> be further developed, the Chinese economy will progress faster in the next decade.

> 若要推广信用卡的使用，必须先建立更加完备的银行法规。
> <u>If</u> [a country] <u>wants</u> to promote the usage of credit cards, establishing more comprehensive bank rules and regulations is a necessary initial step.

4.3 让步 (Concession)

4.3.1 即使……也 (even though ... still)

可以用于真实情况，也可用于纯假设。"即使"一般放在句首，但也可以放在从句的主语之后。口语的说法是"就算……也"。

Can be used in both real situations and unrealistic assumptions. *Jishi* is often placed at the beginning of the first clause, yet sometimes may be placed after the subjective. *Ye* is placed at the beginning of the second clause. The usage is similar to the oral expression "*jiusuan ... ye.*"

> 即使中国实行"一个家庭一个孩子"的政策，也很难抑制人口的大幅度增长。
> <u>Even though</u> China has long been following the policy of "one family one child," it is still difficult for it to reduce the large-scale increase of its population.

4.3.2 纵然……也 (even if ... still)

一般只用于不太可能的情况下的让步。"纵然"可以出现在句首，也可以在从句的主语之后。

Generally used for a situation that is not likely to happen, *zongran* may be placed either at the beginning of the first clause or after the subjective of the first clause.

> 纵然中国实现了在本世纪末把人口控制在十二亿以内的目标，也还是世界上人口最多的国家。
> <u>Even if</u> China could realize the goal to maintain its population at 1.2 billion, it would <u>still</u> be the most populated nation in the world.

> 中国足球队纵然取得世界杯的入场券，也不太可能进入第二轮。
> <u>Even if</u> the Chinese soccer team had won the preliminary match to the World Cup, the chance of making the second round would have been slight.

4.3.3 宁 (可) ……也 (不) (would rather ... than)

一些人认为是副词，但可以起连词的作用。"宁可"用在主语之后，"也"用在下半句 (无主句) 句首。

Although is understood as an adverbial structure by some scholars, it functions as a conjunction. *Ning/ningke* is placed after the subjective of the first sentence; *ye/yebu* is placed at the beginning of the second sentence.

> 在生态学家看来，一个国家宁可降低发展速度，也不应该以破坏自然环境为代价而维持高速发展。
> According to ecologists, a country <u>should</u> reduce the speed of development <u>rather than</u> maintain high-speed development at the cost of its natural environment.

> 宁失千军，不失寸土。
> [We] <u>would rather</u> sacrifice the lives of a thousand soldiers <u>than</u> lose a square inch of territory.

4.3.4 尽管……也 (仍然) (although ... yet)

"尽管"可以用在句首，也可以放在主语后边。

Jin'guan may be placed either at the beginning or after the subjective of the first clause.

> 尽管市政府采取了许多措施，仍然未能明显改善这座城市的交通拥挤状况。
> <u>Although</u> the municipal government has enacted many measures, <u>yet</u> it has obviously failed to ease the traffic jams of this city.

4.3.5 任凭 (despite, in spite of)

放在句首。

Placed at the beginning of the first clause.

> 任凭国会的强烈反对，总统仍希望给这个国家以最惠国待遇。
> <u>Despite</u> the strong opposition from Congress, the president still hopes to grant most favorable nation status to that country.

4.3.6 与其……不如 (would rather … than)

和"宁可……也不"相反，后面才是选择。这个说法比"宁可"更书面语化。

Contrary to "*ningke … yebu*," the second clause is the choice. This expression is more typically a written expression than "*ningke … yebu.*"

> 与其束手就擒，不如背水一战。
> [One] <u>would rather</u> make a last attempt to fight <u>than</u> be captured without any struggle.

4.4 转折 (Transition)

4.4.1 固然……但(是) (to be sure, … but/however)

由两个句子组成的复合结构，"固然"通常放在上句的主语之后，"但(是)"则放在下句的最前面。两句的关系可以是肯定—否定，也可以是否定—肯定。

This structure consists of two clauses respectively with *guran* and *dan(shi)*. *Guran* is often placed after the subjective of the first clause while *dan(shi)* is often placed in the beginning of the second clause. The relationship between the two clauses may be either affirmative-negative or negative-affirmative.

> 发展商业固然是件好事，但是不能因此忽视了基础工业的建设。
> <u>To be sure</u>, it is good to develop commerce. <u>However</u>, the construction of the fundamental framework of the industry should not be thereby ignored.

> 张三固然不是合格的人选，但李四恐怕也难以胜任。
> <u>To be sure</u>, Zhang San is not a qualified candidate. <u>However</u>, [I am] afraid that Li Si is not qualified either.

4.4.2 诚然……但是/不过 (to be sure, … yet)

"诚然"意思与"固然"差不多，但通常放在上句的最前面。

Chengran is similar to *guran*, yet it is often placed at the beginning of the first clause.

> 诚然，儒家的经典在将近两千年来一直是科举考试的中心内容；不过，这并不意味着中国的皇帝们真正按照儒家思想统治国家。
>
> <u>To be sure</u>, Confucian classics provided the core contents of the national civil service examination system for nearly two thousand years. It does not mean, <u>however</u>, that Chinese emperors really followed Confucian teachings to run the country.

4.4.3 然而 = 虽然……但是…… (… however)

放在句首。这句话的意思与前一句话相反。

Placed at the beginning of a sentence. The meaning of this sentence is contrary to the prior sentence(s).

> 货币贬值会引起国内消费者的不满。然而，从国际竞争的角度看，这却是一件好事。
>
> A currency devaluation would cause dissatisfaction among domestic consumers. From the perspective of international competition, <u>however</u>, it would be a good thing.

4.4.4 而 (whereas, yet)

表示比较轻微的转折：

1. 可以放在下半句的句首，后边可以跟"却"；
2. 可以放在同一主语的两个动—宾结构之间；
3. 可以放在两个意思相反的形容词之间。

Er indicates a slight transition, and it may be placed at the beginning of the second sentence, or between the two verb-objective structures of the same subjective, or between two opposite adjectives.

> 西医对这种疾病束手无策，而中医却有不少成功的治疗经验。
>
> Western medicine has no way to cure this disease <u>whereas</u> Chinese medicine has quite a few successful experiences in curing it.
>
> 中国许多国营企业至今仍然追求产量而忽视质量。
>
> Nowadays, many state-run businesses of China still emphasize quantity <u>while</u> ignoring quality.
>
> "小而全"的管理方式不可能产生高效率。
>
> This "small-<u>yet</u>-all-embracing" mode of management cannot be of high efficiency.

* "而"的其他用法见 4.1.3。

  For other usage of *er*, see 4.1.3.

4.5 原因 (Cause)

4.5.1 之所以 (the reason why)

放在原因从句的主语之后。

Placed after the subjective of the clause indicating the causes.

> 以往的研究之所以很难取得成果，是由于方法尚待改进。
> The reason why the previous experiments did not attain their goals is because the methods used were needed to be refined.

4.5.2 鉴于 (in consideration)

放在句首。

Placed at the beginning of a sentence.

> 鉴于日本政府所采取的立场，美国政府应考虑对其实施经济制裁。
> In consideration of the position taken by the Japanese government, the American government should consider to invoke economic sanctions.

4.5.3 考虑到 (in consideration)

放在句子的开始。

Placed at the beginning of a sentence.

> 考虑到外国居民越来越多，这座城市设立了第一家英语电视台。
> In consideration of its increase in foreign residents, the city established its first English language television station.

4.5.4 既然 (如此) ……便/就 (since/since such is the case ... should)

"既然"放在从句的开始，"便/就"放在主句的主语后边。

Jiran (ruci) is placed at the beginning of the first clause, *bian/jiu* is placed after the subjective of the second clause.

> 既然如此，经济史家便应该放开眼界，从整个文化背景着眼以求真正能了解经济史。
> Since such is the case, historians of economy should have an open mind and a perspective from the entire cultural contexts in order to really understand history of economy.

4.5.5 由于 (due to, because)

和"因为"差不多，但是更书面语化一些。

Similar to *yinwei*, yet mostly used in written expressions.

> 由于股票的价格连续下跌，投资者更多地投资于不动产。
> <u>Because</u> stock values have continued to decline, investors are putting more money into real estate.

4.5.6 由于……而……

"由于"后面接原因，"而"后面接结果。

Youyu leads the cause, *er* leads the effect.

> 他由于身体不适而未能在考试中取得理想的成绩。
> Because he was ill, he did not obtain high score in the exam.

4.5.7 因……而……

同上。

Same usage as above.

> 他们因分歧无法调和而离婚。
> Because of irreconcilable differences, they were divorced.

4.6 结果 (Effect)

4.6.1 从而 (therefore, thus, hence)

放在下半句的开始。

Placed at the beginning of the second clause.

> 日本同意作出让步，从而给陷入僵局的美日贸易会谈带来了一线希望。
> The Japanese side has agreed to some concessions, and has thus brought hope to the US–Japan trade negotiations which had previously reached an impasse.

4.6.2 因而 (therefore, thus)

放在下半句的开始。

Placed at the beginning of the second clause.

哈佛大学是世界上最著名的大学之一，因而其学费也就特别昂贵。

Harvard University is one of the world's most famous institutions of higher learning. <u>Therefore</u>, its tuition is extremely expensive.

4.6.3 故而 (therefore, thus, hence)

比"从而"和"因而"更书面语化，用法相同。

More typically a written expression than *cong'er* and *yin'er*. The usage is similar.

> 电脑越来越广泛地运用于社会生活的各个方面，故而许多工业化国家都致力于发展电脑制造业。
>
> Computers are more and more widely used in every aspect of life. <u>Therefore</u>, many industrialized countries are making great efforts to develop computer manufacturing.

4.6.4 可见/由此可见 (it is thus clear that)

放在下半句的开始。

Placed at the beginning of the second clause.

> 对方一再提出新的条件，由此可见他们根本没有谈判的诚意。
>
> The other side has raised new conditions once and again. It is thus clear that they are not serious about arriving at an agreement at all.

4.6.5 则 (will)

在条件句后，常放在表示结果的句子的句首。

Placed at the beginning of the second clause which indicates result.

> 隐患不消除，则后果不堪设想。
>
> Had the hidden danger not been removed, the result <u>would</u> have been dreadful to contemplate.

在一些成语中，表示后面将要发生的事情。

Used in some idioms to indicate things that will happen.

> 穷则思变   poverty <u>will</u> give rise to a desire for change
>
> 不进则退   stagnation <u>will</u> result in regression

* "则"的其他用法见 4.1.4。

 For other usage of *ze*, see 4.1.4.

4.6.6 然则 (if such is the case, then)

类似口语的"那么"。

Similar to oral expression *name.*

> 上述研究表明，中国电脑市场的潜力很大。然则更快地开发中文电脑软件是十分重要
> 的。
> The analysis above demonstrates that the potential computer market in China is vast.
> If this is the case, then the faster development of Chinese software is of great significance.

4.6.7 于是 (thus, hence, then)

放在表示结果的句子的句首。

Placed at the beginning of the second sentence that indicates the effect.

> 政府采取了新政策来刺激石油工业的发展，于是石化原料的价格又恢复到三年前的水
> 平。
> The government adopted new policy to stimulate the development of the petroleum
> industry. <u>Hence</u>, the price of petro-chemical materials fell back to the same level of
> three years ago.

4.7 目的 (Purpose)

4.7.1 以便 (in order to)

在两句话组成的复合句中，放在第二句的句首。

Placed at the beginning of the second clause in a compound sentence consisting of
two clauses.

> 中国正在大力发展职业教育，以便提高劳动者的素质，参加国际竞争。
> China is doing its best to develop continuous education <u>in order to</u> improve the quality
> of labor and to fare well in international competition.

4.7.2 以使 (in order to, in order that)

在两句话组成的复合句中，放在第二句的句首。

Placed at the beginning of the second clause in a compound sentence consisting of
two clauses.

> 政府应当加强对新技术研究的投资，以使企业真正具有国际竞争力。

The government should strengthen its investiments in the research in new technology <u>in order for</u> the enterprises to really have the ability to compete on an international basis.

4.7.3 以免 (in order to avoid)

在两句话组成的复合句中，放在第二句的句首。

Placed at the beginning of the second clause in a compound sentence consisting of two clauses.

> 研究者应该进行广泛的调查，以免作出错误的结论。
> The research should involve a large-scale investigation <u>so that</u> the wrong conclusion can <u>be avoided</u>.

4.7.4 以 (in order to)

放在第二句的句首，可以看成"以便"的省略。

Placed at the beginning of the second clause, can be understood as the abbreviation of *yibian*.

> 历史上日本曾派出大批"遣唐使"来中国，以学习中国的先进文化。
> According to history, Japan sent many "envoys to the Tang dynasty court" <u>in order to</u> learn about the advanced culture of China.

4.7.5 以期 (so as to, expect to)

放在第二句的句首。

Placed at the beginning of the second clause.

> 上海正在加强浦东地区的基本建设，以期有更多的外商来此投资。
> Shanghai is strengthening infrastructure construction in Pudong region so as to attract more foreign investments.

4.7.6 为 (了) (in order to)

放在句首。"为了"在口语和书面语都常用，"为"则主要用于书面。

Placed at the beginning of a sentence. *Weile* is used in both written and spoken expressions while *wei* is mainly used in written expressions.

> 为打击毒品走私活动，中国政府决定加强同国际刑警组织的合作。
> <u>In order to</u> crack down on drug smuggling, the Chinese government has decided to strengthen the cooperation with the International Police Anti-crime Organization.

第 五 章 • 介 词 和 介 词 词 组
Chapter 5 • Prepositions and Preposition Phrases

现代汉语中书面语中的介词是学生的难点之一，因为很多介词的用法和口语不同。本章将逐一讨论介词的用法。

In the written expressions of modern Chinese, the usage of prepositions or prepositional phrases is one of the most difficult areas for students because many of them are quite different from spoken expressions.

5.1 之

5.1.1 的 (of)

主要用于一些习惯性的短语中，如"之后"、"之中"、"之间"、"之上"、"之下"、"之行"、"之风"等等。

In modern Chinese, *zhi* is mainly used in some idioms such as *zhihou* (after), *zhizhong* (in, within, among), *zhijian* (between, among), *zhishang* (above), *zhixia* (under), *zhixing* (visit by), *zhifeng* (the custom of).

> 美国总统的中东之行并未产生重大的影响。
> The US President's Middle East <u>visits</u> did not have a great impact.

> 改革之后，中国的贪污之风泛滥成灾。
> After the reform started, <u>waves of</u> corruption overwhelmed China.

5.1.2 双音节名词 + "之" + 单音节形容词 (double-character noun + *zhi* + single-character adjective)

作主语，有强调的意思。也可以理解为把形容词名词化。

Used as an emphasized noun phrase. Can also be understood to turn adjective into noun.

> 这次商品展销会的品种之多，质量之好，是近年来少有的。

Merchandise of such a large quantity and good quality in this exhibition/sale show has rarely been seen in recent years.

5.2 所

5.2.1 主语 + "所" + 动词 + "的"(+ 动作对象) (subjective + *suo* + verb + *de* (+ objective))

放在动词的前面，在古汉语中代表动作的对象，但是在现代汉语中常常与代表的事物同时使用。

Suo is placed before the verb of the noun phrase. In classical Chinese, it represents the objective of the action. In modern Chinese, however, it is often used together with the thing it represents.

> 他所说的都是实话。/他所说的话都是真的。
> All that he said was true.
>
> 孔子所关注的是人们道德的堕落，而不是经济的进步。
> What Confucius was concerned about was the the decline of the people's morality, not the progress of its economy.
>
> 我们所讨论的问题具有很重要的实际意义。
> The problem we are discussing has great significance in practice.

5.2.2 成语或短语 (in idioms)

> 所谓   so-called
>
> 为所欲为 = 想干什么就干什么   do whatever one wants to do
>
> 不知所云 = 不知道说的是什么   do not understand what one said

5.3 为

5.3.1 (第二声)动词 + "为" + 表示身分、地位、职务、状态的名词 (verb + *wei* + noun that indicate status, position, occupation, or state)

5.3.1.1 成为 (become)

> 中国要使上海重新成为世界贸易的中心。
> China wants to make Shanghai a center of world trade again.

5.3.1.2 变为 (turn into)

在短短的几年内，深圳由一个小镇变为一座现代化的大城市。
In a short period of just a few years, Shenzhen <u>turned into</u> a modern metropolis.

5.3.1.3 选为 (elected as)

他被选为这个工厂的厂长。
He has been <u>elected as</u> the director of this factory.

表示变化的动词和"为"还可以组成四字或六字短语。结构是：动词 + 名词/形容词 + "为" + 名词/形容词。如果前面的名词是单音节的，后面的也应该是单音节。如果前面的名词或形容词是双音节的，后面也应该是双音节。

The verbs indicating change and transformation plus *wei* can make phrases of four or six characters. The structure is verb + noun/adjective + *wei* + noun/adjective. If the noun or adjective in the fore is a single character, the rear one should be a single character too; if it is double-character, the rear one should suit.

变废为宝   <u>turn</u> waste <u>into</u> treasure

化悲痛为力量   <u>turn</u> sorrow <u>into</u> strength

5.3.2 (第二声) 用在动词之后，表示"当作"的意思 (used after the verb, meaning "as")

苏联解体后，美国将中国视为主要的对手。
After the disintegration of the former Soviet Union, the United States started to regard China <u>as</u> the main rival.

5.3.3 (第二声)"为" + 名词 + "所" + 动词 (*wei* + noun + *suo* + verb)

这里的"为"和"被"的意思相近。

In this pattern *wei* functions as *bei.*

多年来，中国的改革一直为通货膨胀所困扰。
For many years, China's economic reform has been complicated by inflation.

这种产品深为欧美消费者所喜爱。
This product is deeply loved by American and European consumers.

这种理论早已为实践所证明是行不通的。
Pracitce has long proved that this theory won't work.

5.3.4 （第二声）副词 + "为" + 双音节动词 (adverb + *wei* + double-character verb or adjective)

雷锋的故事在六十年代广为流传。
In the 1960s, the story of Lei Feng became widely known.

对国会的决议，白宫深为不满。
The White House is extremely unhappy about the decision made by Congress.

5.3.5 （第四声）为……而 (for the sake of)

"为"后面可以接表示目的的词语，也可以接表示原因的词语，"而"后面接动词。在一些情况下，"而"可以省略。

Wei is followed by words either indicating purpose or indicating causes; *er* is followed by verb. In some cases, *er* can be omitted.

中国人民正在为现代化而奋斗。
Chinese people are striking <u>for</u> modernization.

我们为他的成功而感到自豪。
We are truly proud of his success.

毛泽东反对"为艺术而艺术"。他认为，文学艺术应当为工农兵服务。
Mao Zedong objected to "art for art's sake." He believed that literature and art should serve for workers, peasants, and soldiers.

5.3.6 （第四声）为……起见 (for the sake of)

表示目的。

Indicate purpose.

为保险起见，他建议请专家审议后再将方案付诸实施。
<u>For the sake of</u> safety, he suggests that the plan be carried out after the experts' inspection.

5.4 就

5.4.1 就……而言/论/看 (in terms of)

就思想的深度而论，宋代儒学大大超过了汉代儒学。

<u>In terms of</u> the depth of philosophical quest, Song Confucianism surpassed Han Confucianism greatly.

5.4.2 "就" + 宾语 + 双音节动词 (*jiu* + objective + double-character verb)

双方就贸易问题举行了两个小时的会谈。
The two sides conducted formal discussions on trade for two hours.

两国就交换留学生达成了协议。
The two countries reached an agreement regarding the exchange of students.

5.5 对于 (to, in)

口语中常用"对"，意思相近。
Similar to *dui* in oral expression.

有人认为孔子对于经济的发展不感兴趣，其实，这是一种误解。
Some people believe that Confucius was not interested <u>in</u> economic development. In fact, this is a misunderstanding.

5.6 在……中 (in, among)

表示以有明确界定的空间或时间为特点具体的东西和有过程中的抽象的事物。口语中更多用"里"来代替"中"。

Used for things with definite space or time, or for things with a process. *Li* is more frequently used in oral expression than *zhong*.

这位教授的做法在校园中引起了轩然大波。
What this professor did caused great disturbance on the campus.

在调查过程中，意想不到的情况接二连三地发生。
Unexpected events occured one after another <u>during</u> the investigation.

* 会议或类似会议的情况常常既可以用"在……上"，也可以用"在……中"。
For conference, meeting, etc., both *shang* and *zhong* can be used.

在这次会议上 / 中，他提出了一个惊人的建议。
<u>During</u> the meeting, he made a surprising proposal.

5.7 于

5.7.1 与动词或省略系动词"是"的形容词配合使用（verb + *yu* or adjective (to function as verb) + *yu*）

5.7.1.1 善于（be good at）

他善于在最困难的时候找出解决问题的方法。

He is <u>good at</u> finding a way out at the most critical moment.

5.7.1.2 精于（be good at），拙于（be weak in）

这位画家精于山水而拙于人物。

This painter is <u>excellent at</u> "mountain-river" scenarios but <u>weak in</u> portraits.

5.7.1.3 严于（be strict with）

国家领导人应该严于律己。

A state leader should be <u>strict with</u> himself.

5.7.1.4 利于/有利于（be helpful in）

发展太阳能利于减少污染。

To develop solar energy will be <u>helpful in</u> reducing pollution.

5.7.1.5 适于（be suited to）

这种机器适于在农村使用。

This kind of machines are <u>suited to</u> rural areas.

5.7.1.6 敢于（dare to）

在关键时刻，他敢于挺身而出，这实在难能可贵。

He really deserves praise for his <u>courage to</u> step forward at the critical juncture.

5.7.1.7 用于（be used in/for）

这个说法主要用于书面语。

This phrase is maily <u>used in</u> written expressions.

5.7.1.8 忙于（be busy with）

政府的官员忙于为自己建造高级别墅，根本不管老百性的死活。

The government officials were <u>busy with</u> building luxury estates for themselves and did not care about the life of the common people at all.

5.7.1.9 便于 (be convenient for)

政府以"便于管理"为借口，强迫农民到指定的区域出售农副产品。
Under the pretext of "<u>convenience to</u> manage," the government drove peasants to sell their products within designated areas.

5.7.1.10 惯于 (be accustomed to)

这位外交部长惯于在谈判的最后阶段提出对方难以接受的要求。
This foreign minister is <u>used to</u> making tough requests that his opponent can hardly accept in the last phases of negotiation.

5.7.1.11 过于 (be excessive in)

由于在外贸政策方面过于谨慎，这个国家的工业失去了一个扩大出口的良机。
Because of overcaution in its policies regarding foreign trade, this country's industry lost a good chance to increase its exports.

5.7.1.12 限于 (be limited by)

限于篇幅，本书只能对此事件作简要介绍。
<u>Limited by</u> space, the present work can only make a brief account of this event.

5.7.1.13 在于 (lies in)

很多外国专家认为中国农业的根本出路在于机械化。
Many foreign experts believe that the fundamental way to improve China's agriculture <u>lies in</u> mechanization.

5.7.1.14 处于 (be in/at)

这个国家的经济处于最困难的阶段。
The economy of this country is in the most difficult stage.

5.7.2 于 = 对于

新经济政策于国于民有百害而无一利。
For the country and the people, the new economic policy has hundreds of disadvantages without a single advantage.

5.7.3 于 = 在

常常用于新闻报导。

Mostly used in news report.

中国共产党第十五次代表大会将于明年初召开。
The 15th Congress of the Chinese Communist Party will be held early next year.

中韩两国外长谈判定于十九日在汉城举行。
The discussion between Chinese and Korean ministers is scheduled <u>on</u> 19th at Soeul.

5.8 以

5.8.1 放在单音节动词后面 (placed after single-character verb)

5.8.1.1 加以

这个历史事件非常重要，值得加以认真研究。
This historical event is very significant and worthy of careful study.

5.8.1.2 给以

可以分开使用。
Gei and *yi* can be separated.

对于群众的积极性，政府应当给以大力支持。
For the dynamism of the people, the government should show great support.

两国的联合行动给恐怖主义组织以沉重的打击。
The cooperative action of the two countries dealt the terrorist organizations a heavy blow.

5.8.1.3 处以

他主张对这名罪大恶极的杀人犯处以极刑。
He insisted on pushing this murderer to death for his heinous crime.

5.8.2 以……来 (use … to, to … by means of)

"以"有"用"的意思，表示手段，"来"后面接动词。
Here, *yi*'s meaning is similar to *yong*, indicating means of action. *Lai* is followed by a verb.

很多总统候选人都以减税的承诺来争取选民的支持。
Many president candidates attracted voters by promising to reduce taxes.

以商业来促进工业发展的做法在这个国家很难成功。

In this country, to stimulate industrial development by increasing commercial activities will be difficult to implement.

一些教授主张以汉语拼音来代替国语注音符号。

Some professors propose to replace the Chinese phonetic mark (bo-po-mo-fo) system with the Pinyin system.

5.8.3 以……为 = 把……当作/作为 (to regard … as, to consider … as)

以转口贸易为特徵的新加坡近年来也加强了基础科学的研究。

In recent years, Singapore, whose economy is characterized by entrepôt trade, has also emphasized the study of basic science.

三千年前，黄河流域的居民以小米为主要的粮食作物。

Three thousand years ago, the residents of the Yellow River valley mainly lived on millet.

5.8.4 以……而言/论 = 就……而言/论 (in terms of)

以国画的内容而论，可以分为山水、花鸟、人物等几大类。

In terms of contents, Chinese paintings can be classified according to the following categories: mountain-river, plant-animal, and portrait.

5.8.5 以……居多/为多 (… as the majority)

与会者以共和党人居多。

Most of the attendees in this meeting were Republicans.

5.9 除……(以)外 (Except)

口语中常用"除了……(以)外"，书面语中两种说法都有。应该注意，汉语中的"除(了)……以外"有两种意思。

Both "*chule … (yi)wai*" and "*chu … (yi)wai*" can be used in written expression while only the former is used in oral expression. One should be aware that this expression has two different meanings as noted below.

5.9.1 除……(以)外，还…… (besides)

出席会议的除政府部长外，还有主要国营企业的代表。

Besides government ministers, representatives from major SOEs (State-owned enterprises) also attended this meeting.

5.9.2 除……(以)外，……都/均…… (all … except …)

除日本外，亚洲各国都反对商业捕鲸。
Except for Japan, all the other Asian coutries object to commercial whaling.

5.10 至

5.10.1 由/从……至…… = 从……到…… (between … and …)

由北京至天津的公路十分拥挤。
The highway <u>between</u> Beijing and Tianjin is very crowded.

5.10.2 至此 (by now)

至此，俄军从阿富汗撤出的计划已全面完成。
<u>By now</u>, the plan to withdraw Russian troops from Afghanistan has been completed.

至此，这个国家结束了原油依赖进口的历史。
<u>By now</u>, this country has ended its history of relying solely on imported petroleum.

5.10.3 至于 = 关于 (as for)

人们都认为中国应该控制人口的增长。至于如何实现这个目标，则有很多不同的见解。
All believe that China should control its population growth. <u>As for</u> how to realize this goal, they have many different opinions.

5.10.4 乃至 (even to)

这种产品在中国乃至整个亚洲都很有名。
This product is not only famous in China, but <u>even to</u> the rest of Asia.

5.11 经 (After, Through, Via)

经全体委员讨论决定免除他的北京市市长职务。
After discussion, the members of the committee decided to dismiss him from the position of mayor of Beijing.

江泽民主席圆满结束了对中亚三国的工作访问，昨经乌鲁木齐返京。
President Jiang Zemin successfully completed his working visit to the three Central Asia countries and returned to Beijing <u>via</u> Wulumuqi.

张某因伤势过重，经抢救无效死亡。

Despite the efforts of paramedics, Zhang died due to his serious injury.

第 六 章 · 疑 问
Chapter 6 • Interrogation

6.1 何

"何"是古代汉语中最常用的疑问词，现代汉语的书面语保留了一些古代汉语的用法。

He is the most common word of interrogation in classical Chinese. This usage is preserved in the written expressions of modern Chinese.

6.1.1 如何 = 怎样 (how)

可以用于疑问句，但更多是用于引导主语和宾语从句。

Can be used in interrogative sentences but for most cases, it is used to lead subjective or objective clauses.

> 如何减少对进口能源的依赖，是台湾面临的最大问题之一。
> The biggest problem Taiwan faces is <u>how</u> to reduce its dependence on import energy.

> 来自世界各地的代表正在讨论如何控制环境污染以及保护野生动物等一系列重大问题。
> Representatives from all over the world are discussing a series of significant issues, such as <u>how</u> to control environmental polution, and <u>how</u> to protect wild animals.

6.1.2 何在 (what is)

放在句末，前面一般是双音节词语。

Mainly placed at the end of a sentence, often after a two-character phrase.

> 这位作者一直强调中国是下个世纪最大的不稳定因素，请问理由何在？
> This author insists that China will be the biggest element leading to world instability in the next century. [We have to] ask: <u>What is</u> the reason?

> 日本的一些人宣称日本在一九三一年侵略中国东北是合法的，我们不禁要问，这些人居心何在？

Some Japanese claim that the Japanese invasion of Manchuria was legal. We cannot help to ask: <u>What is</u> the purpose of their claim?

6.1.3 为何/缘何 = 为什么 (why)

后面接双音节或四音节动词词组。"缘何"是比"为何"更古典的说法。

Often before two-character or four-character phrase. *Yuanhe* is more classical.

> 美国为何对此议案行使否决权？
> <u>Why</u> did the United States veto this bill?

6.1.4 有何 = 有什么 (what)

后面接双音节词。

Often before a two-character word.

> 记者纷纷询问总统在重新当选后有何计划？
> Many reporters asked the president of <u>what</u> his plan will be after re-election.

> 上述计划有何不妥，敬请指示。
> Please give us instruction about <u>whatever</u> is improper in the above-mentioned proposal.

6.1.5 何尝 = 哪里曾经 (whenever)

> 我们何尝不想停止军备竞赛，但是邻国的武器更新换代使我们不得不增加国防开支。
> <u>How could</u> we <u>not</u> wish to stop military competition? However, the artillery upgrades of neighboring countries give us no other choice but to increase defense expense.

6.1.6 何曾 = 哪里曾经 (whenever)

> 这位思想家何曾主张过言论自由？
> <u>Whenever</u> did this thinker insist on freedom of speech?

6.1.7 何时 = 什么时候 (when)

> 中国何时才能实现电脑普及化？这个问题很难回答。
> <u>When</u> will China popularize computers? It is a difficult question to answer.

6.1.8 何处/方 = 什么地方 (where)

> 请问何处可以买到适用于苹果机的中文软件？
> May I ask <u>where</u> I can find Chinese software for Macintosh computers.

6.2 否 (not)

从表面上看，"否"是一个表示否定的词语，但是在现代汉语中，"否"主要用为疑问词。

The basic meaning of *fou* is negation. In modern Chinese, however, *fou* is mainly used as an interrogative word.

6.2.1 能否 = 能不能 (can or cannot)

后边接双音节动词。

Followed by double-character verb.

> 能否给与协助？盼速答复。
> <u>Can</u> you give us assistance? We are eager to hear your reply.

> 能否在任期内提高人民的生活水平将决定这位总理的命运。
> <u>Whether</u> this premier can improve the people's standard of living within his term of office will decide his future.

> 电脑能否提高学习外语的效率？对此专家们有非常不同的看法。
> <u>Can</u> computer heighten the efficiency of foreign language learning? Experts have expressed quite different opinions.

6.2.2 与否 = 是还是非 (or not)

前面是双音节的动词或形容词。

After a double-character verb or adjective.

> 这种看法的正确与否，还要看实践的检验。
> Practice will prove <u>whether or not</u> this opinion is correct.

> 老师讲课时应注意学生理解与否。
> A teacher should pay attention to <u>whether</u> her students understand her or not.

6.2.3 形容词 + "否" (adjective + *fou*)

一般是单音节形容词。

Generally, the adjective should be of single character.

> 以上处理方式当否，请予以指示。
> Please tell us <u>whether</u> the above-mentioned solution is appropriate <u>or not</u>.

6.2.4 是否 = 是不是 (be or not)

一般放在动词前面。

Generally placed before a verb.

> 国会正在讨论是否修订宪法的问题。
> The Congress is discussing <u>whether or not</u> an amendment to the constitution is needed.

6.3 岂 (how could)

常见的词组有"岂能"、"岂可"、"岂非"、"岂容"等。

Often appears in such compound words as below:

6.3.1 岂容 (how could [we] allow)

> 中国领土岂容侵略者横行？
> <u>How could</u> [we] allow intruders to run wild in Chinese territory?

6.3.2 岂能 (how could)

> 岂能将现代中国与秦始皇的时代混为一谈？
> <u>How could</u> it be possible to confuse modern China with time of the First Emperor of the Qin regime?

6.3.3 岂可 (how could)

> 此事关系重大，岂可草率决定？
> This is a grave matter. <u>How could</u> it be decided in a rush?

6.3.4 岂非 (how could it not be)

> 日本一些人把教科书中的"侵略中国"改为"进入中国"，岂非别有用心？
> The Japanese Ministry of Education changed the textbook description of "invading China" to "entering China." <u>How could</u> there not be an ulterior motive?

第七章·否定与双重否定
Chapter 7 · Negation and Double-negation

7.1 未 = 没有 (Not)

7.1.1 单独使用 (when used independently)

放在动词前面。

Placed before verbs as a negative adverb.

> 凡未经卫生部批准的药品，不得在市场上出售。
> Any medicine <u>not yet</u> approved by the Ministry of Public Health may not be marketed.

7.1.2 从未 = 从来没有 (never)

> 两国从未发生过边境冲突。
> There has <u>never</u> been a boundary conflict between the two nations.

7.1.3 未曾 = 没有（做过）(never)

> 他未曾访问中国，却对中国的情况了如指掌。
> Although he has <u>never</u> been to China, he knows Chinese affairs like the back of his hand.

7.1.4 未必 = 不一定 (not necessarily)

> 采用新技术未必能够解决这个国家的经济危机。
> Adopting new technology <u>cannot necessarily</u> solve the economic crisis this country faces.

7.1.5 未免 (a bit too)

> 你们对于西藏问题的看法未免太幼稚了。
> Your opinion on Tibetan issue is <u>a bit too</u> naive.

7.2 不 (Not)

7.2.1 从不 = 从来不 (never)

这位教授从不与政客交往。

This professor has <u>never</u> been in contact with politicians.

7.2.2 不曾 = 没有 (never, did not)

因为行程匆忙，我们不曾参观著名的历史博物馆。

Because of our busy schedule, we <u>did not</u> visit the famous Museum of History.

7.2.3 毫不 = 一点也不 (not at all)

虽然面对强大的国际压力，该国领导人毫不动摇地坚持原来的政策。

In spite of great international pressure, the leaders of this country insisted on maintaining the previous policy <u>without</u> wavering.

7.2.4 不外 (no other than)

局势的进一步发展不外两种可能性。

The further development of the present situation is <u>no more than</u> two possibilities.

7.2.5 不无 = 有一些 (双重否定) (double negative)

遭受挫折对一名年轻运动员说来不无助益。

For a young athlete, it is not unhelpful to suffer some losses.

7.2.6 不妨 (there's no harm to try)

既然别的方法都不见效，不妨试试这种特别的方法。

Since other means have no effects at all, <u>it is no harm to</u> try this special method.

7.3 无 (No)

7.3.1 毫无 = 一点也没有 (not at all)

对于这场突如其来的暴风，香港的居民毫无准备。

Surprised by this storm, Hong Kong residents had made <u>no</u> preparations at <u>all</u>.

7.3.2 无非 (no more than, nothing but)

佛教的这些理论，无非是让人们从尘世的痛苦中解脱出来。
These Buddhist tenets preaches <u>nothing but</u> liberation from the worldly afflictions.

7.3.3 无从 (do not know where to start doing something)

我们感到问题太多，无从谈起。
We feel there are so many problems that we do not know <u>where to</u> start our speech.

7.3.4 无异 (于) (no difference with)

这样做无异于搬起石头砸自己的脚。
To do so is <u>just like</u> lifting a rock only to drop it on one's own feet.

7.3.5 无外 (乎) (have no other than, no more than)

形势的发展无外乎三种可能性。
There are no more than three possibilities for the further development of the situation.

7.4 莫 (Not)

7.4.1 切莫 = 千万不要 (do not)

用在命令句。
Used in imperative sentences.

在发生火灾的时候，切莫慌乱。
<u>Do not</u> panic should there be a fire.

在成绩面前切莫骄傲。
<u>Do not</u> be arrogant in front of success.

7.4.2 且莫 = 先不要 (not to do something for a while)

用在命令句。
Used in imperative sentences.

且莫对这个事件下结论，我们需要做更多的调查。
<u>Do not</u> make a hurry conclusion since we need more detailed investigation.

7.4.3 莫过于 (no more than)

该市居民最担心的莫过于空气污染问题。
The great*est* concern of the residents of this city is air pollution.

7.5 非 (Not)

7.5.1 并非 = 并不是 (not)

我们抵制日货并非针对日本人民，而是反对其政府的贸易保护主义政策。
Our boycott of Japanese goods <u>is not</u> an action against the Japanese people, but the protectionist policies of its government.

减少政府开支并非解决经济危机的灵丹妙药。
To reduce government expenses <u>will not</u> provide a panacea for the economic crisis.

7.6 勿 = 不要 (Not)

用在命令句。

Used in imperative sentences.

请勿吸烟。
No smoking.

第八章 • 时间词语
Chapter 8 • Time Words and Phrases

现代汉语书面语中的时间状语的表达方式同口语有比较明显的差别，需要专门加以讨论。

The written expressions of time adverbials of modern Chinese are often quite different from oral expressions, and therefore need special attention.

8.1 基本时间 (Basic Time Expressions)

8.1.1 季 (seasons)

口语的春天、夏天、秋天、冬天在书面语中常常用春季、夏季、秋季、冬季，或者只说春、夏、秋、冬。

When seasons are mentioned in written expressions, *tian* is often replaced with *ji* or omitted.

> 他于一九九四年秋赴美深造。
> In the fall of 1994, he went to the United States to further his academic pursuit.
>
> 夏秋两季　the two seasons of summer and fall
>
> 去冬今春　from the winter of last year through the spring of this year

8.1.2 日 (date)

书面语不用"号"只用"日"。

Hao is replaced with *ri* in written expressions.

8.1.3 时分 (time)

> 凌晨　　before dawn
>
> 清晨　　time around 6 to 7 p.m.
>
> 晨＝早上　morning

正午	12 noon
午后	afternoon
晚 = 晚上	evening
午夜	midnight

8.1.4 时 (o'clock)

书面语不用"点"而用"时"。口语中的"X点多"在书面语中用"X时许"来表达。

For hours, *dian* and *duo* are respectively replaced with *shi* and *xu* in written expressions.

> 十日下午四时许。
> A little after four in the afternoon.

8.1.5 分 (minute)

书面语，尤其是新闻报道，一般不用"半"，不用"刻"，也不用"差几分"或者"过几分"的表达方法，只说"某时某分"。

Generally, such terms as "half (hour)," "quarter," "X minute to" or "past X o'clock" are not used in written expressions, especially in news reports.

> 上午十时五十九分，江泽民主席来到人民大会堂。
> President Jiang Zemin came to the Great Hall of the People at 10:59 a.m.

8.1.6 昨天 (yesterday)、今天 (today)、明天 (tomorrow)

书面语常常省略为昨、今、明，特别是在作修饰语时。另外，书面语在特别正式的新闻报道中也用昨日、今日、明日的说法。

In writing, *tian* is often omitted for these three words, especially when they are used as modifiers. In addition, formal news reports also replace *tian* with *ri*.

> 中国代表团明日赴纽约参加联合国大会。
> The Chinese delegation will leave for New York tomorrow to attend UN assembly.

8.2 简单时间词 (Simple Time Words)

除非特别说明，下面的词是作状语用。

If not specified, they are adverbs or, in other words, used to modify verbs.

8.2.1　现在或最近 (now/recent)

8.2.1.1　此刻/此时/此时此刻 (at this moment)

可以独立作状语，也可以修饰名词。

Can be used to modify either the action or a noun.

> 此刻，他的心情极为激动。
> At this moment, he was extremely excited.

8.2.1.2　当今/当前/当下 (at present)

> 当前的主要任务是发展电子工业。
> The primary task <u>at present</u> is to develop electronic industry.

8.2.1.3　时下/现今/现下 (nowadays)

> 时下，减肥饮食很流行。
> <u>Nowadays</u>, fad diets are popular.

8.2.1.4　近日 (recent, future)

这个词的用法非常特别，既可以表示过去几天，也可以表示未来几天。

A very unique word which can indicate either several days ago or several days later.

> 记者从近日召开的全国石油工业会议获悉，中国去年开发大型油田二十三个。
> From the national working meeting of petrolem oil which was held several days ago, the reporter got the news that during the last year China developed 23 large-sized oil fields.

> 中国青年代表大会将于近日召开。
> The National Conference of Chinese Youth will be held in a few days.

8.2.1.5　近来 = 最近以来 (recently)，近年来 = 最近几年来 (in recent years)

> 近来，国内电子产品市场非常活跃。
> <u>Recently</u>, domestic electronic market has been booming.

> 近年来，两国加强了经济合作。
> <u>In recent years</u>, the economic cooperation between the two countries has been reinforced.

8.2.1.6　日前 (yesterday/a few days ago)

> 日前召开的全国工业会议的主要议题是如何增加出口。
> The national conference on industry held yesterday focused on how to increase exports.

8.2.2 过去 (past)

8.2.2.1 往日/昔日/往昔 (the past days/bygone days)

主要用来修饰名词。

Mainly used to modify nouns.

> 动乱过后，这座城市恢复了往日的平静。
> After the turmoil, stillness was restored to the city.

8.2.2.2 以往 (previous, previously)

> 切莫忘记以往的教训。
> Do not forget the <u>previous</u> lessons.

> 以往，人们常常认为绿色对眼睛有益，最近的一些科学家提出了相反的看法。
> <u>Previously</u>, people often believed that the color green is good for the eyes. But recently some scientists have suggested the contrary.

8.2.3 将来或过去将来 (future or future in the past)

8.2.3.1 翌日/翌年 (the next day/next year)

> 两位总统的会谈定于翌日举行。
> The formal meeting of these two presidents will be held <u>tomorrow</u>.

> 翌日，他在日本外相的陪同下赴京都访问。
> The <u>next day</u>, he visited Kyoto, accompanied by the Japanese foreign minister.

> 他在翌年的朝鲜战争中丧生。
> He died in the Korean War which started in the <u>next year</u>.

8.2.3.2 即将 = 快要 (soon)

> 第四十三届联合国代表大会即将召开。
> The 43rd session of the UN general assembly <u>will soon</u> begin.

8.2.3.3 来年 (next year, future)

> 这项工程能否上马要根据来年的经济形势而定。
> Whether this project can be started or not <u>will</u> be decided by next year's economic situation.

8.2.3.4 他日 (some other time)

> 此问题极为复杂，可留待他日解决。
> This problem is very complicated and [we] may wait till some other time to solve it.

8.2.3.5 日后 (in the future)

此问题如不尽快解决，日后必生枝节。

If the problem remains unsolved, it will certainly bring more troubles in the future.

8.2.4 立刻 (immediately)

8.2.4.1 当即/随即/即刻 (right away)

鉴于海湾战争爆发，政府决定即刻取消飞往该地区的所有航班。

At the outbreak of the Gulf War, the government dicided to immediately cancel all the flights to that area.

8.2.4.2 及早/尽早 (as soon as possible)

修饰动词，主要用在命令或建议中。

A modifier to a verb, used mainly in commands or suggestions.

这个问题应尽早解决。

This problem should be solved as early as possible.

8.2.4.3 速/火速

修饰动词，主要用在命令或建议中。

A modifier to a verb, used mainly in commands or suggestions.

你部应火速驰援该地区。

Your unit should rush to that area to support [our forces there].

8.2.5 永久 (ever)、经常 (often) 或重复 (repeatedly)

8.2.5.1 历来/一向/始终 (always)

用来修饰动词，强调从过去到现在一直不变。

A modifier to a verb, stressing the state of being unchanged from the past to the present.

中国一向支持南南合作。

China always supports South-South cooperation (cooperation among third world countries).

这个国家始终未能摆脱对进口石油的依赖。

This country has never gotten rid of dependence on imported petroleum.

农业历来是该国的经济支柱。

For that country, agriculture <u>has been</u> the main pillar of its economy.

8.2.5.2 不时 (frequently)

参观时，他不时提问，并作了许多笔记。

During his visit, he frequently asked questions and made a lot of notes.

8.2.5.3 时常 (often)

居京期间，他时常到城南的旧书店购书。

During his stay in Beijing, he often went to the used-book stores in the southern part of the city.

8.2.5.4 每每 (time and again)

常用于否定的意义。

Often has a negative meaning.

人们每每将二者混为一谈。

People time and again confuse these two things as one.

8.2.5.5 平素/素 (来) ＝ 平常 (normally, usually)

这两位文坛巨子平素很少来往。

Seldom did these two great masters of literature visit each other.

8.2.5.6 通常 (often)

治理污染的效果通常需要几年的时间才能显示出来。

The effects of pollution control will <u>often</u> take several years to become obvious.

8.2.5.7 连日 (来) (day after day)

工人和学生连日来举行声势浩大的游行示威。

Workers and students staged large-scale demonstrations <u>for the last few days</u>.

8.2.5.8 屡/屡次/屡屡 (repeatedly)

会议中，他屡次提出修改宪法的问题。

During the meeting, he <u>reiterated</u> the issue of constitution amendments.

8.2.5.9 一再/再三 ＝ 反复 (repeatedly)

总统一再强调发展同中国关系的重要性。

The president <u>reiterated</u> the significance of developing a closer relationship with China.

对方一再破坏临时停火协议，使我们不得不怀疑其谈判的诚意。
The other side's <u>repeated</u> breach of the cease fire agreement makes us doubt about their sincerity for negotiation.

外交部长对美国的经济援助再三表示感谢。
The foreign minister <u>repeatedly</u> expressed thanks for the US economic aid.

8.2.5.10 轮番 = 一次又一次 (one after another)

敌军出动大量飞机对我阵地轮番轰炸。
The enemy deployed a great number of airplanes to bomb our position.

8.2.6 有时 (sometimes, occasionally)

8.2.6.1 偶或/间或/偶尔 = 有时候 (occasionally)

这位作家的作品主要反映渔民的生活，偶尔也有对城市生活的描写。
The works of this author are mostly reflections of the life of fishermen. <u>Sometimes</u> he also describes urban life.

8.2.7 完成或未完成 (completion or incompletion)

8.2.7.1 已 = 已经 (already)

口语中用"已经"，书面语则多用"已"。

Different from oral expressions, written expressions often replace *yijing* with simply *yi*.

大选已近。
The general election is <u>coming</u>.

经济形势如此严峻，仅仅靠借款已无济于事。
The economic situation is so serious that it would <u>already</u> be useless to rely only on loans.

8.2.7.2 至今/迄今 = 到今天 (hetherto, so far)

该市的交通和环境污染问题至今尚无明显改善。
<u>So far</u> the traffic and environmental problems of that city have not yet been improved.

对于癌症的研究已经有数十年的历史，但迄今尚未发现疗效十分显著的抗癌药。
Cancer research has a history of several decades. However, the researchers have <u>not yet</u> found a medicine which is obviously effective in curing the disease.

8.2.8 还是 (still)

8.2.8.1 仍 = 仍然 (still)

虽然政府三令五申，乱收费现象仍屡禁不绝。
Although the government <u>reiterated</u> its prohibition, the incidents of arbitrary charge/overcharge still cannot be stopped.

8.2.8.2 依然/依旧 (still)

对方依然坚持令人无法接受的条件。
The other party still insists on these unacceptable conditions.

三十年过去了，但这里的风光依旧。
Although 30 years have passed, the scene here is still the same as it was before.

8.2.8.3 犹 (still)

常用于四字结构中。

Often used in four-character structures.

失败了两次，他心犹不甘。
After failing twice, he still does not want to give up.

8.2.9 最后 (at last)

8.2.9.1 终 (finally)

这项计划终因财政困难而未能实现。
This plan finally failed due to financial difficulties.

8.2.9.2 迟早 (sooner or later)

这场风波迟早要发生。
Sooner or later, this disturbance would necessarily happen.

8.3 复合时间短语 (Compound Time Phrases)

8.3.1 甫……即…… (as soon as)

外长甫下飞机即前往白宫晋见美国总统。
The foreign minister went to the White House to meet the US president as soon as he got off his airplane.

8.3.2 ……间 = 在……中间 (amid …)

席间，乐队演奏了两国民间音乐。
During the banquet, musicians played the folk music of the two countries.

8.3.3 临……前 (right before …)

临行前，他在机场发表了书面讲话。
Before leaving this country, he delivered a written speech at the airport.

8.3.4 ……前夕 (on the eve of …)

解放前夕，周某全家移居香港。
Right before liberation (1949), Zhou's whole family immigrated to Hong Kong.

8.3.5 ……以降 (after …)

春秋以降，礼乐制度发生了巨大的变化。
After the Spring and Autumn period, great changes had taken place in rites and ceremonies.

8.3.6 ……在即 (shortly)

秋收在即，应准备好有关农用物资。
The fall harvest is <u>coming soon</u>, thus the farming materials and equipment should be made ready for it.

8.3.7 (在)……期间 (during)

考生在考试期间不得离开考场。
Examinees are not allowed to leave the examination room <u>during</u> the examination.

8.3.8 ……时 = ……的时候 (when)

读历史小说时应注意，小说中的描述可能与史实不完全一致。
<u>When</u> one reads a historical novel, one should be aware that the description in the novel is not necessarily identical with historical facts.

遇到困难时且莫垂头丧气。
Don't be frustrated <u>when</u> encountering difficulties.

8.3.9 继······之后 = 在······以后 (after ...)

杨逵是继赖和之后的又一位杰出代表。
Yang Kui is another eminent representative <u>after</u> Lai He.

毋庸置疑，孟子是继孔子之后儒家的最重要的代表人物。
Without doubt, Mencius was the most important figure of Confucianism <u>after</u> Confucius.

继"九一八"事件占领中国东三省之后，侵华日军又策划了"七七"事变。
<u>After</u> the "September 18 Incident" which led to the Japanese occupation of three northeastern provinces of China, the Japaneses army planned a "July 7 Incident."

8.3.10 (值此)······之际 (on this occasion of ...)

值此新春之际，我谨代表国家教委祝贺大家春节愉快。
<u>On this occasion of</u> the Chinese New Year celebration, I, on behalf of the State Commission of Education, wish you all a happy new year.

8.3.11 ······之前 = 在······以前 (before)

试验之前，他阅读了大量有关资料。
<u>Before</u> the experiment, he read a lot of relevant information.

8.4 年龄 (Age Related Words)

8.4.1 对某些年龄的文学表述 (literary expressions for certain ages)

年方二八	16 years old
年未若冠	younger than 20
而立之年	30 years old
不惑之年	40 years old
年过半百	over 50
年过花甲	over 60
年逾古稀	over 70

8.4.2 享年X岁 (died at the age of X)

金山先生昨日在京逝世，享年八十七岁。
Mr. Jin Shan passed away in Beijing yesterday at the age of 87.

第九章 • 程度修饰语
Chapter 9 • Degree Modifiers

9.1 有些 (Some)

9.1.1 有所 = 有一些 (somehow)

后面一定是双音节的不及物动词，放在句末。

Must be followed by a double-character intransitive and placed at the end of a sentence.

> 有所察觉　to have somehow noticed
>
> 有所了解　to have some knowledge of
>
> 有所提高　to have some increase/improvement

9.1.2 略 = 有些 (some)

> 对于这位哲学家的论点，我略知一二。
> I have <u>some</u> familiarity with the opinions of this philosopher.

9.2 大部分 (Most)

9.2.1 大都 = 大部分 (mostly)

> 他的作品大都描写天津工人的生活。
> <u>Most</u> of his works describe the life of Tianjin workers.

9.2.2 几乎 = 差不多 (almost)

> 由于电脑的普及，几乎没有人再使用打字机了。
> Due to the widespread use of computers, <u>almost</u> nobody uses typewriters anymore.
>
> 市场上的电视机和录像机几乎都是日本产品。
> <u>Most</u> TV sets and video recorders are made by Japanese companies.

9.2.3 大抵 (generally)

该公司生产的新款太阳能汽车与传统汽车的售价大抵相同。
The solar energy automobiles newly designed and manufactured by that company are sold at roughly the same prices as traditional ones.

9.3 都 (All)

9.3.1 均 = 都 (all, both)

这种新药对于肝炎和肾炎均有疗效。
This new medicine is effective for <u>both</u> hepatitis and nephritis.

9.3.2 皆 = 都 (all)

这种新型的连锁商店在大中城市皆可看到。
This kind of new chain stores can be found in <u>all</u> the big and mid-sized cities.

9.3.3 全然 (thoroughly)

日本全然不顾国际舆论的谴责，继续进攻上海。
Ignoring international condemnation, Japan continued to attack Shanghai.

9.4 很 (Very)

9.4.1 大为 = 大大的 (greatly … by …)

后面接双音节不及物动词。
Followed by double-character intransitive.

看了这篇小说后，我大为感动。
I am <u>greatly</u> moved <u>by</u> (reading) this novel.

9.4.2 极为 (尤为) = 非常，特别是 (extremely, especially)

后面接双音节不及物动词。
Followed by double-character intransitive.

汉代的长袖舞和巾舞也是极为发达的，女子长袖对舞尤为发达。

The long-sleeve dance and handkerchief dance were also very advanced during the Han Dyansty, <u>especially</u> the lady's long-sleeve pair dance.

政府对学生的行动极为不满。

The government is <u>extremely</u> unhappy with the activities of students.

9.4.3 颇 = 很 (very)

两国代表对建立跨国公司的设想颇感兴趣。

The representatives of these two countries are <u>very much</u> interested in the proposal to establish a transnational corporation.

我们对超级大国的霸权主义颇为反感。

We <u>strongly</u> detest the hegemony of the superpowers.

9.4.4 殊 (quite)

中国队能取得此成绩，殊出意料。

It was <u>quite</u> unexpected that the Chinese team could make such an achievement.

9.4.5 甚 (very)

我们对贵方的安排甚为满意。

We are <u>very</u> satisfied with the arrangement of your side.

9.5 越来越 (More and More)

9.5.1 越发 = 越来越

随着时间的推移，这种应急措施的缺陷越发明显。

With the passage of time, the disadvantages of this temporary expedient become <u>more and more</u> obvious.

9.5.2 愈加 = 越来越

近年来，中东局势愈加紧张。

In recent years, the tense situation in the Middle East has become <u>graver</u>.

9.5.3 日益 (increase day by day)

近来，要求治理污染的呼声日益高涨。

Recently, the call for proper management of pollution has become <u>stronger and stronger</u>.

9.6 绝对 (Absolute)

9.6.1 断 (然) (decisively)

中国代表断然拒绝了这种无理要求。

The Chinese representative decisively refused such an unreasonable demand.

第十章·数量的表达方式
Chapter 10 • Quantitative Expressions

10.1 基本数量单位 (Basic Units of Numbers)

汉语的基本数量单位是个、万、亿、兆，同英美的千、百万不同。但是在一些科学文章中，有时会以千为基本单位，例如十千、一百千等等。

The fundamental units of the Chinese numeric system are *wan* (ten thousand), *yi* (hundred million), and *zhao* (trillion). In some scientific writings, however, such expressions as *shiqian* and *yibaiqian* are used.

10.2 序数词 (Ordinals)

10.2.1 "其" + 数字 (*qi* + number)

其一 = 第一　first

其二 = 第二　second

10.2.2 "首先"、"其次"、"再次"

首先 = 第一　first

其次 = 第二　second

再次 = 第三　third

10.3 分数 (Fractions)

10.3.1 顺序 (order)

说法与英文相反，先说分母，再说分子。

In Chinese expression of fractions, the denominator always comes before the numerator. This is the opposite of English expression.

三分之一   1/3

五分之二   2/5

10.3.2 强和弱 (more and less)

在分数中，强和弱分别表示多和少。

In fraction, *qiang* and *ruo* respectively denote "more" and "less."

10.3.2.1 强 = 比……还多 (more than)

四分之一强   More than one-fourth

10.3.2.2 弱 = 比……少一些 (less than)

三分之一弱   Less than one-third

10.4 百分数 (Percentage)

10.4.1 百分数的高和低的表达方法 (expressions for high or low percentage)

形容百分数很高常用"高达"或"多达"，形容百分数很低一般用"仅占"。

To mention a high percentage, *gaoda* (as high as) or *duoda* (as many as) are the most often used words. *Jinzhan* (only make up) is usually used to describe a low percentage.

这个国家的通货膨胀率高达百分之一百五十。
The inflation rate of this country is <u>as high as 150%</u>.

多达百分之七十的居民反对扩建飞机场。
<u>As many as 70% of the residents</u> submitted objections to the airport expansion project.

中国成年人口中受过高等教育的仅占百分之二。
<u>Only 2% of Chinese adults</u> receive higher education.

10.4.2 百分点 (lit., percentage point)

一个百分点等于百分之一，通常只用于低于20%的百分数。

One *baifendian* equals 1%. Often used for below 20%.

上半年的通货膨胀率只增加了三个百分点。

The inflation rate in the first half of the year was <u>as low as 3%</u>.

10.4.3 成 (1/10, 10%)

今年的夏粮可望增长三成。

The increase in summer crops is expected <u>to be 30%</u>.

10.5 比例 (Proportion/Ratio)

10.5.1 比例的描述 (description of proportion)

可以用"大"和"小"，也可以用"高"和"低"。

Either *daxiao* or *gaodi* can be used for description of proportion.

该市的外来人口占很大 (高) 的比例。

<u>A large proportion</u> of that city's population are immigrants.

10.5.2 成 (不成) 比例 (in/out of proportion)

如果车辆的增加和道路的建设不成比例，势必造成严重的交通阻塞。

If the increase of vehicles and road construction are <u>out of proportion</u>, serious traffic jams will be inevitable.

10.5.2.1 成正比 (direct proportion)

工资的提高和购买力的增长成正比。

An increase in salary and an increase of purchasing power are in <u>direct proportion</u>.

10.5.2.2 成反比 (inverse proportion)

在现代社会，生活水平的提高通常同人口的出生率成反比。

In modern society, the improvement of the standard of living and the birth rate are often <u>inversely proportional</u>.

10.6 比较 (Comparison)

10.6.1 增加 (increase)

三年来，学习中文的人数以每年百分之十的速度递增。

During the past three years, students of the Chinese language have <u>increased by 10% each year</u>.

与五年前相比，该地区的犯罪率上升了百分之八十。
As compared to five years ago, the crime rate of this region <u>increased by 80%</u>.

第三季度同第二季度相比，电脑的销售量增长了百分之十五。
As compared to the second quarter, the computer sales in the third quarter <u>increased by 15%</u>.

菲律宾的劳务输出由一九七六年的三万九千人猛增到一九八三年的三十万人。
The Philippine's labor exports <u>rapidly increased</u> from 39,000 in 1976 to 300,000 in 1983.

东亚国家的移动电话的用户两年中激增了百分之二百。
The users of cellular phones in East Asia have <u>dramatically increased</u> by 200% in two years.

10.6.2 减少 (decrease)

"希望工程"使这一地区的失学率下降到百分之二。
"Hope Project" has <u>reduced</u> the dropout rate of students in this region <u>to 2%</u>.

由于严重的自然灾害，去年的香蕉产量减少了二成五。
Due to severe natural disasters, last year's banana crop decreased by 25%.

与去年同期相比，重大交通事故降低了百分之四十三。
As compared to the corresponding period last year, major traffic accidents dropped by 43%.

世界经济的不景气使我国上半年的出口额下跌了二十个百分点。
Due to the worldwide economic depression, our country's exports dropped by 20% in the first half of this year.

国际经济制裁使该国的石油出口锐减百分之八十。
International sanctions made that country's petroleum exports decrease sharply by 80%.

10.6.3 倍数 (multiples)

中国的倍数表达常常给人以误解。例如，"增长了三倍"可能指是原来的百分之四百，但也可能是原来的百分之三百。

The Chinese expressions of multiples are often misleading. For example, *zengzhang le sanbei* may mean either three times the original amount or four times the original amount.

在过去的十五年中，人均国内产值提高了2.1倍（由5,008美元增到10,428美元）。

The GDP per capita has increased by 2.1 times in the past 15 years (from 5,008 dollars to 10,428 dollars).

人均电力需求在同期内增加了4.3倍（由132千瓦时增到562千瓦时）。

The electricity demand per capita has increased by 4.3 times during the same period (from 132kwh to 562kwh).

10.6.4 相当于 (equivalent to)

一九八八年"四小龙"对东盟国家的投资多达48.6亿美元，已相当于日本同年对该地区投资的89.4%。

The investment of the "Four Little Dragons" in ASEAN countries reached as much as $4.86 billion in 1988, or 89.4% of Japanese investment to the same region in the same year.

10.6.5 超过 (surpass)

十大建设工程的投资额超过五十八亿美元。

The investments in the ten largest construction projects surpass $580 million.

10.6.6 以上 (more than, over)

香蕉出口占该国总出口额的百分之四十以上。

Banana exports account for over 40% of the total exports of that country.

10.7 长度 (Length)

中国传统的长度单位已被官方废止，国际通行的公制取而代之。但是在日常生活中旧制仍然为人们所使用。

China has a traditional system for length units. Although this system was officially abandoned and replaced by the metric system, it is still used in daily life.

10.7.1 传统的长度单位 (traditional length units)

里　500 m

丈　3.3 m

尺　0.33 m

寸　　0.033 m

分　　0.0033 m

10.7.2　公制（Metric system）

公里(km)　　1000 m

米(m)　　1 m

分米(dm)　　0.1 m

厘米(cm)　　0.01 m

毫米(mm)　　0.001 m

10.8　重量（Weight）

中国的传统的重量单位中最重要的是"斤""两"和"钱"。原来一两是十六分之一斤，后来中国大陆把一斤变成了十两，但是中药以及金银等的重量仍然按照旧制。现在这两种旧制都已被官方废止而通行公制。

The most important weight units in traditional Chinese system are *jin*, *liang and qian*. Previously, 1 *liang* was 1/16 *jin*. Later, the conversion was changed to 1 *liang* equals 1/10 *jin*. For Chinese medicine and the jewelry industry, however, the old system remained unchanged. Now, both systems were abandoned and replaced by the Metric system.

10.8.1　市制（traditional system）

斤　　500 g

两　　50 g/31.25 g

钱　　5 g/3.125 g

10.8.2　公制（Metric system）

克　　1 g

公斤　　1 kg

吨　　1000 kg

10.9 面积 (Area)

中国传统的面积单位中最重要的是"亩"、"分"和"厘"。现已废止而通行公制。

The most important area units in traditional Chinese system are *mu*, *fen*, and *li*. This system was already abandoned and replaced by the Metric system.

10.9.1 市制 (traditional system)

亩   666.67 m²

分   66.67 m²

厘   6.67 m²

10.9.2 公制 (Metric system)

平方公里   1,000,000 m²

平方米   1 m²

平方分米   0.01 m²

平方厘米   0.0001 m²

10.10 近似的量 (Estimation)

10.10.1 上下/左右 (around)

该国的年度经济增长率一直保持在百分之六上下。
That country's economic growth rate remains <u>around</u> 6% per year.

10.10.2 接近 (近) (close to)

印度的人口已接近十亿。
The population of India is already close to one billion.

在民意测验中，他领先对手近四个百分点。
According to the survey, he has about a 4% advantage over his rival.

10.10.3 约 (approximately)

日本新材料市场的规模目前大约是三兆日元(约合一百九十亿美元)。

The present scale of the new material market in Japan is valued about 3 trillion Japanese yen (approximately 19 billion US dollors).

10.11 其他与量有关的词汇 (Other Terms Regarding Quantity)

净   net

净重   net weight

净增   net increase

净利   net profit

毛重   gross weight

毛利   gross profit

10.12 书面语的特殊量词 (Special Measure Words Used Only in Writing)

书面语常常要求使用比口语更加精致和准确的量词而较少用"个"。下面是一些主要用于书面而不常用于口语的量词。

Written expressions often require more refined and accurate measure words and avoid using *ge*, the "universal" measure word. The following are some examples of the measure words mainly used in written expressions.

10.12.1 名 (for people of certain categories)

三百馀名近视眼患者   over 300 myopia patients

10.12.2 席 (for a long speech)

一席语重心长的话语   a speech with sincere and earnest consideration

10.12.3 番 (for speech or performance)

一番丑恶的表演   an ugly show up

10.12.4 计 (for beat or blow)

一计重扣   a heavy blow (in volleyball or other sports)

10.12.5 部 (for works, masterpieces)

两部获得国际大奖的中国电影　two Chinese movies with grand international awards

10.12.6 客 (for meals)

一客午餐　a lunch

10.12.7 起 (for incident, accident, or criminal case)

三起事故　three accidents

10.12.8 曲 (for eulogy in an abstract sense)

一曲共产主义的颂歌　a communist eulogy

10.12.9 则 (for news)

新闻二则　two pieces of news

10.12.10 株 (for trees)

一株松树　a pine

第十一章·独立短语
Chapter 11 • Independent Phrases

11.1 表示总结或概括 (Conclusion or Generalization)

11.1.1 总之/总而言之 (in general, generally speaking)

总而言之，一个国家的经济发展不能完全依赖另外一个国家。

In general, the economic development of a country cannot be completely dependent on another country.

11.1.2 一言以蔽之 = 用一句话来概括 (in one word/sentence)

一言以蔽之，美国在人权问题上对中国的批评不过是为了阻止中国成为下个世纪的超级强国。

In one word, the criticism of China by the United States on the issue of human rights is merely an attempt to prevent China from becoming a superpower in the next century.

11.1.3 综上所述 = 综合上面所说的话 (to sum it up)

综上所述，道家同儒家在许多方面存在着根本的分歧。

To sum it up, there are discrepancies in many aspects between Daoism and Confucianism.

11.1.4 大体而言 = 从最主要的方面看 (generally speaking)

大体而言，预期寿命可以作为衡量国民健康水平的主要尺度。

Generally speaking, the expected human life span may serve as the major measure in judging the level of national health.

11.2 表示肯定 (Confirmation)

11.2.1 毫无疑问 (undoubtedly)

毫无疑问，日本的电子工业在世界上首屈一指。

Without a doubt, the electronic industry of Japan is the most advanced in the world.

11.2.2 无庸置疑 (beyond doubt)

无庸置疑，美国仍然是世界上军事力量最强大的国家。
<u>Beyond doubt</u>, the United States is still the strongest military power in the world.

11.2.3 不应否认 (should not be denied)

不应否认，改革使大多数中国人的生活水平提高了。
<u>It should not be denied</u> that economic reforms have heightened the standard of living for most of Chinese people.

11.2.4 显而易见 (obviously)

显而易见，日本的反对党并不希望对美日关系做根本调整。
<u>Obviously,</u> the opposition party of Japan does not want to make a rapid change in the relationship between Japan and the United States.

11.2.5 众所周知 (as well known to all)

众所周知，亚洲的大部分国家都面对人口压力。
<u>As well known to all</u>, most Asian countries are facing the pressure of overpopulation.

11.3 表示另外一层意思的开始 (To Start a New Meaning)

11.3.1 此外 (in addition)

此外，杜甫的论艺诗也相当具有新意。
<u>In addition</u>, Du Fu's poems on art critics also show originality.

11.3.2 与此同时 (meanwhile)

八十年代末期，该国经济开始为通货膨胀而困扰；与此同时，贪污腐败也成为严重的社会问题。
During the end of the 1980s, the economy of that country started to suffer from inflation. <u>Meanwhile</u>, corruption became a serious social problem.

11.4 表示意思等同 (Same or Similarity)

11.4.1 亦即 (i.e., that is)

石化产品，亦即以石油为主要原料的化学工业产品，是这个国家的主要发展目标。

Petro-chemical products, <u>i.e.,</u> the chemical products made mainly from petroleum, are the priority for development in this country.

11.4.2 换言之 (in other words)

董仲舒主张独尊儒术。换言之，他主张以儒家思想作为国家的唯一指导原则。
Dong Zhongshu insisted on paying respect only to Confucianism. <u>In other words</u>, he proposed to hold to Confucian thought as the only guideline of the country.

11.5 表示进一步 (Further)

11.5.1 更有甚者/犹有甚者 (some even go much further)

这个国家的许多人认为西方的政治制度不适用于他们的国家。更有甚者，最近出版的一本书宣称，只有恢复帝制才能使国家安定。
Many people of this country believe that the Western political systems are not suited to their country. <u>Some even go much further</u>. A recently published book claims that the restoration of the imperial system is the only way to make the country stable.

11.6 举例 (Example)

11.6.1 譬如 = 比方说 (for example)

战国末期各种思想派别之间的相互影响非常明显。譬如，儒家的荀子就吸收了道家的很多概念和理论。
The mutual influence between different schools of thought became obvious during the end of the Warring States period. For example, Xun Zi, the great master of Confucianism, adopted quite a few concepts and ideas from Daoism.

11.6.2 试举一例 (now [I] try to illustrate it with an instance)

同为儒家的代表人物，孟子和荀子之间有许多分歧。试举一例，在人性理论方面，两位思想家的看法几乎完全相反。
Both as representatives of Confucianism, Mencius and Xun Zi expressed many differences. On the theory of human nature, for instance, their concepts are almost completely opposite.

第 十 二 章 • 成 语
Chapter 12 • Classical Idiomatic Phrases

现代汉语的习惯短语可以分为两组：成语和俗语。成语通常来自古书，大部分是四个字，在书面语和比较正式的口语中常常使用。俗语大部分是大众的现代创造，三个字的比较多，主要在日常会话中使用。

The idiomatic phrases of modern Chinese can be divided into two groups: *chengyu* or classical idiomatic phrases and *suyu* or vernacular idiomatic phrases. The classical idiomatic phrases are often rooted in ancient texts. Most of them consist of four characters, and they are frequently used in written discourse and formal conversation. By contrast, the vernacular idiomatic phrases are basically created by common people in modern time. Many of them consist of three characters and are mainly used in daily conversations.

12.1 成语的功能和语用规则 (Functions of Classical Idiomatic Phrases and Their Grammatical Rules)

虽然大多数成语只有四个字，但是结构相当复杂。比如"愚公移山"这个成语，就包括了主语 (愚公)、动词 (移) 和宾语 (山) 这三种成分。但是成语作为固定的词组，其功能并不完全由其自身结构所决定。比如愚公移山这个成语在现代汉语中主要是用作修饰名词的形容词。下面是成语的一些典型的功能以及相关的语法规则。

Although most of the classical idiomatic phrases consist of only four characters, their structures may be quite complicated. For example, the classical idiomatic phrase *yugong yishan* is composed of a subject (*yugong*, Foolish Old Man), a verb (*yi*, move) and an object (*shan*, mountains). In actual use, however, an idiomatic phrase often forms a single grammatical unit whose internal structure does not necessarily determine how the unit will function. Still taking *yugong yishan* for instance, it is mainly used as an adjective, or a modifier to a noun. The following are some typical functions of the classical idiomatic phrases and their respective grammatical rules.

12.1.1 用作表语 (used as predicate)

很多成语可以放在联系动词"是"的后边作表语。"是"的前边可以有"真"或者"实在"

等副词起强调作用。除了"是"以外，书面语的词组"无异于"和"岂非"等也用作联系动词，后面可以接成语。

Most classical idiomatic phrases can be placed after the link verb *shi* to form a predicate. Adverbs such as *zhen* or *shizai* can be used before *shi* for emphasis. Besides *shi*, such written expressions as *wuyiyu* (none other than), and the rhetorical *qifei* (is that not) also function as link verbs, and can therefore be used before classical idiomatic phrases.

12.1.2 用作独立短语 (used as independent phrase)

有一些成语本身是完整的一句话，不需要添加任何其他成分，例如"民不聊生"等等。

Some classical idiomatic phrases may function as complete sentences, and can be used by themselves (without addition of any other words). *Minbuliaosheng*, "people do not have means of making a living," is one example of this type.

12.1.3 用作动词 (used as verb)

不少成语可以用作动词。在这些成语中，有一些可以直接放在主语之后，另外一些只能放在"应该"、"要"、"会"、"可以"等助动词之后。

Many classical idiomatic phrases may function as verbs. Some of them can be placed directly after the subject while others must follow an auxiliary verb such as *yinggai* (should), *yao* (need), *hui* (will), or *keyi* (may).

一般而言，成语作动词时后边不能再加宾语，要指明宾语需将其放在动词的前面，并且由"对"等介词来引导。

Generally speaking, when a classical idiomatic phrase functions as a verb, it cannot be followed by an object. To specify the object, one must place it before the verb and set it off with a preposition such as *dui*.

半信半疑 (half-believe and half-doubt)：

✗ 我半信半疑他。

✗ 我半信半疑他的话。

✓ 我对他半信半疑。

✓ 我对他的话半信半疑。

✓ 听了他的话，我半信半疑。

12.1.4. 在"话题—评论"结构中作评论语 (used as comment in "topic-comment" structure)

很多成语可以在"话题—评论"结构中作评论语。作为评论语的成语的前后不应添加任何其他成分。例如，在"两书的内容大同小异"这句话中，"两书的内容"是话题，成语"大同小异"作评论。

Many classical idiomatic phrases can be used as comments in "topic-comment" structure. When the classical idiomatic phrase acts as a comment, no additional words or phrases should be placed before or after it. For example, in the sentence "*liangshu de neirong datong xiaoyi*," idiomatic phrase "*datong xiaoyi*" (basically the same with only minor differences) acts as a comment on the topic "*liangshu de neirong*" (contents of the two books).

12.1.5 用作形容词 (used as adjective)

有些成语可以用作形容词。当一个成语作形容词修饰名词的时候，在成语和名词之间一定要有"的"或者"之"。

Some classical idiomatic phrases can be used as adjectives. When a classical idiomatic phrase as an adjective modifies a noun, there must be a *de* or *zhi* between the classical idiomatic phrase and the noun it modifies.

有些成语作为形容词可以放在"得"的后面做补语，表示程度。

As adjectives, some classical idiomatic phrases can be placed after *de* as a complement, indicating degree.

无论是修饰名词还是作补语，成语前边一般不应该加"很"、"非常"等表示程度的副词。这和汉语的其他形容词常常要求"很"等副词来修饰形成了鲜明的对照。

In general, adverbs such as *hen* and *feichang* that express degree should not be used in front of a classical idiomatic phrase no matter whether it modifies a noun or functions as a complement. By contrast, many adjectives other than the classical idiomatic phrases often require such adverbs preceding them.

12.1.6 在动词前作副词用 (used as adverb to modify verb)

有些成语可以作修饰动词的副词，此时，成语和动词之间一定需要"地"。

Some classical idiomatic phrases can be used as adverbs. In such a case, there must be a *de* between the classical idiomatic phrase and the verb.

12.1.7 用作名词 (used as noun)

一些成语主要用作名词，在句子中作主语或者宾语。

Some classical idiomatic phrases are mainly used as nouns, and in a sentence, such a phrase can act as either the subject or the object.

从构成的性质上看，成语可以分为典故性、比喻性、结构性三种。下面，按照这种分类将现代汉语书面语最常用的一些成语作简要介绍。每个成语后面括号中标出的是该成语的主要功能。

In accordance with their natures of formation, classical idiomatic phrases can be divided into story-based idioms, analogous idioms, and structural idioms. Following this classification, we list below some classical idiomatic phrases that are frequently seen in modern written Chinese, and briefly explain their meanings. The major grammatical functions of each of these phrases are marked in parenthesis: adj = adjective, adv = adverb, c = comment, iph = independent phrase, n = noun, p = predicative, v = verb.

12.2 典故性成语 (Story-based Idioms)

典故性成语有非常明确的历史背景。如果不知道成语背后的故事，就很难理解成语的意义。故而本组成语的英文翻译我们先给出故事，然后再翻译其意义。

A story-based classical idiomatic phrase involves an allusion to a historical event or literary text. To understand each idiom, one has to know the story behind it. Thus, in translating these phrases, we shall briefly introduce the stories and then explain their meanings.

12.2.1 班门弄斧 (adj, adv, p, v)

Story : A carpenter used an axe to show off his woodworking skill in front of the home of Lu Ban (a great carpenter of the early Warring States period who was later worshipped by Chinese carpenters as the founder of their profession).

Meaning: To display one's scanty knowledge in the presence of a great expert.

> 在这位名家面前，你不要班门弄斧。
> Do not show off your scanty knowledge in the presence of that famous expert.

12.2.2 草木皆兵 (adj, p, v)

Story: In a battle, a defeated general was so scared that he mistook every bush and tree for an enemy soldier.

Meaning: To be in a state of extreme nervousness.

> 你不要草木皆兵。反对你的人并不多。
> Do not mistook every bush and tree for your enemy. In fact, you do not have many adversaries.

12.2.3　此地无银三百两 (adj, iph)

Story: A man hid 300 taels of silver in a certain place and then put up a sign there saying "No 300 taels of silver buried here."

Meaning: Conspicuously protesting one's innocence reveals that one is guilty.

> 该组织"此地无银三百两"的声明恰恰暴露了他们参与了这次事件。
> That organization's statement which conspicuously pleads their innocence just reveals their involvement in this incident.

12.2.4　邯郸学步 (adj, p, v)

Story: A man who appreciated the walking style of Handan (a city in North China) people went there to learn how to walk. Finally, however, he not only failed to imitate the Handan people, but lost his own ability to walk also.

Meaning: Failing in both learning from others and reserving one's own ability.

> 豆腐是中国的发明，但是现在有些中国人到日本去学习怎么做豆腐，这不是邯郸学步吗？
> Tofu is an invention of China. However, some Chinese are now going to Japan to learn how to make tofu. Is that the same as the man who lost his own ability to walk by learning from the people of Handan?

12.2.5　画龙点睛 (adj, p)

Story: Immediately after a painter put in the pupils of the eyes of a painted dragon as the finishing touch, it was brought to life and flew away.

Meaning: Adding the vital finishing touch.

> 此文的最后一段，堪称画龙点睛之笔。
> The last paragraph of this article can be appreciated as a vital finishing touch.

12.2.6　井底观天 (adj, p, v)

Story: A frog living at the bottom of a well thinks that the sky is the same size as the mouth of the well.

Meaning: Very limited and provincial attitude.

> 这种井底观天的态度使该国在国际竞争中处于劣势。
> This provincial attitude made that country inferior in international competition.

12.2.7　滥竽充数 (adj, p, v)

Story: In a massive band, some pipe players were just pretending to play while others were actually playing.

Meaning: Fill position just to make up the number.

> 他认为大多数国会议员都是滥竽充数。
> He believes that most congressmen are just filling up positions without doing any real work.

12.2.8　破釜沉舟 (adj, p, v)

Story: A commander ordered his soldiers to break their cauldrons and sink their boats after they had advanced across a river to wage a decisive battle.

Meaning: Cutting off all means of retreat.

> 杜尔破釜沉舟，辞去议员职务，希望在大选中击败克林顿。
> Cutting off all means of retreat, Dole resigned from his position as senator, hoping to defeat Clinton in the presidential election.

12.2.9　杞人忧天 (adj, p, v)

Story: A man from the state of Qi worried about the collapse of heavens.

Meaning: Unnecessary worries.

> 很多经济学家认为环境主义者的警告无异于杞人忧天。
> Many economists believe that the warnings of environmentalists are nothing more than groundless worries.

12.2.10　黔驴技穷 (v)

Story: When a donkey was brought to Qian, where no donkey had ever been seen before, it scared a tiger by neighing and kicking. Finally, however, the tiger discovered that the donkey had no further skills and killed it.

Meaning: One's poor skills get exhausted.

日本军国主义已经黔驴技穷。

The Japanese militarists' poor skills have got exhausted.

12.2.11 守株待兔 (adj, p, v)

Story: A man observed a hare run into a tree stump and die one day, so he waited there the next day hoping another hare would run into the stump.

Meaning: Wait for a most unlikely windfall.

坐等国际援助无异于守株待兔。

To do nothing but to wait for international aid is no different from holding out for a highly impossible stroke of luck.

12.2.12 四面楚歌 (adj, p, v)

Story: The Lord of Chu was besieged by the forces of his rival. When he heard the songs of Chu coming from the enemy encampments that surrounded him, he lost hope, believing that most of his country men had surrendered.

Meaning: Be opposed by people on all sides, including even one's previous allies.

由于坚持增税，这位总理陷入四面楚歌的境地。

Because of his persistence in raising taxes, this prime minister has been opposed by people from all sides.

12.2.13 他山之石 (n)

Story: Although the stones of one hill cannot be used to polish jade, those from another hill may work.

Meaning: One may benefit from other region's experience, advice, etc.

我们应该把别国的经验作为他山之石，加以认真研究，来解决我们自己面临的问题。

We should take the experiences of other countries and carefully study them in order to solve the problems we are facing.

12.2.14 胸有成竹 (adj, adv, p, v)

Story: When a painter was asked why he painted bamboo faster and better than others, he replied that he was so familiar with bamboo that it was almost as though the bamboo were part of his body.

Meaning: Have great confidence in doing something because of one's long preparation.

教练胸有成竹地说："我们一定能夺得冠军。"

With full confidence, the coach said, "We will surely win the championship."

12.2.15 叶公好龙 (adj, p, v)

Story: The Duke of Ye was known for being fond of dragons. He decorated every corner of his house with dragons. When a real dragon came, however, he became terrified.

Meaning: Professed love of what one really fears.

这位政治家总是高谈改革，但是对于大家提出的改革措施却百般阻挠，可见他对于改革只是叶公好龙。

This politician always talks about reform. However, he has done his utmost to obstruct the concrete steps for reform proposed by others. In spite of his professions, it is clear that he does not really support reform.

12.2.16 夜郎自大 (adj, c, p, v)

Story: Yelang was a small isolated state but its king believed the territory under his government was very large. When he was visited by an envoy from the Han dynasty, he was so ignorant of his country's relative status as to ask arrogantly which country was larger.

Meaning: Ludicrous conceit.

任何国家都不应该夜郎自大。

No country should be blindly arrogant.

12.2.17 愚公移山 (adj)

Story: A man with the name of Foolish Old Man had a home surrounded by several high mountains. Feeling that the mountains were an inconvenience, he decided to remove them by digging day by day. His action was mocked by another man with the name of Clever Old Man. But God was moved by the determination of the Foolish Old Man and helped him to remove the mountains.

Meaning: Keep working hard to achieve a goal that seems impossible.

我们要以愚公移山的精神来建设国家。

We should work toward the reconstruction of our country with the spirit of the "foolish old man" who tried to move mountains.

12.2.18 朝秦暮楚 (adj, p)

Story: A man who served as a minister of Qin in the morning shifted his allegiance and became a minister of Chu in the evening. (Qin and Chu were the most powerful states during the Warring States period.)

Meaning: Unbelievably quick to switch sides.

> 这位政客朝秦暮楚的行为使人们非常反感。
> That politician's quickly switching sides is detested by the people.

12.2.19 坐收渔利 (adj, p, v)

Story: When a snipe and a big clam became involved in a struggle with each other, a fisherman easily got both of them.

Meaning: Profit by others' conflicts.

> 该国希望两个邻国之间的冲突升级，这样它就可以坐收渔利。
> That country hoped that the conflicts between its two neighbors would escalate so that it could profit from.

12.2.20 一鸣惊人 (adj, adv, p, v)

Story: After three years' silence in a cage, a bird made a brilliant chirping that surprised its owner.

Meaning: Make one's mark at the first shot.

> 中国队一鸣惊人，取得了这次比赛的冠军。
> As a dark horse, the Chinese team obtained the championship.

12.3 比喻性成语 (Analogous Idioms)

比喻性成语是用形象化的比喻来说明一定的道理或者描述一定的状态。在翻译本组成语时，我们先直译，以显示其比喻的本来面目，然后再翻译其意义。

The analogous idioms use analogies based on visual imagery to explain certain ideas or to describe certain states. In translating this group of phrases, we have first provided a literal translation, which gives the original image, and have followed this with an explanation of the image's meaning.

12.3.1 百花齐放 (adj, c, p)

Literal translation: A hundred kinds of flowers bloom together.

Meaning: A great number of different opinions/styles are thriving and competing with each other.

> 八十年代末期，该国的文学创作曾经出现百花齐放的局面。
> A proliferation of literary creation from a wide varieties of different schools and styles was seen in this country during the late 1980s.

12.3.2 拔苗助长 (adj, p, v)

Literal translation: Try to help the shoots grow faster by pulling them upward.

Meaning: Spoil things by excessive zeal/impatience.

> 很多中国家长采取了拔苗助长的态度来对待自己的孩子。
> Many Chinese parents' attitude towards their children is like trying to help the shoots grow by pulling them upward.

12.3.3 得寸进尺 (adj, adv, p, v)

Literal translation: Seeking a foot after gaining an inch.

Meaning: Very greedy.

> 日军得寸进尺，在侵占东北以后，又向华北进攻。
> Seeking a foot after gaining an inch, the Japanese army advanced to attack North China after they occupied Manchuria.

12.3.4 风马牛不相及 (adj, c, p)

Literal translation: Even in mating season a mare would have nothing to do with a bull.

Meaning: Two things are totally unrelated.

> 这位教授认为，基础教育同环境保护并非风马牛不相及。
> This professor believes that the elementary education and environment preservation are not totally unrelated.

12.3.5 画蛇添足 (adj, adv, c, p, v)

Literal translation: Draw a picture of a snake and add legs to it.

Meaning: Ruin the effect by adding something superfluous.

> 这个方案已经相当完善，我劝你不要画蛇添足。
>
> This plan is almost perfect. I advise you not to ruin it by adding something superfluous.

12.3.6 九死一生 (adj, c, p)

Literal translation: The odds of dying are 9 to 1.

Meaning: Very dangerous.

> 探险队员都知道，他们此行九死一生。
>
> All the members of the exploration team knew that the dangers ahead were so great that they had only a slim chance of returning.

12.3.7 举棋不定 (adj, p, v)

Literal translation: A chess player picks up a piece but does not know where to place it.

Meaning: Hesitate to make a move.

> 该党领导人在关键时刻举棋不定，导致大选惨败。
>
> The leader's hesitation in the critical moment left that party miserably defeated in the general election.

12.3.8 举足轻重 (adj, c, p)

Literal translation: A man is standing at the center of a balance, and a slight move of his feet will result in imbalance.

Meaning: Play a decisive and balance-holding role.

> 此项工程举足轻重，一定要考虑周到。
>
> Since this project is the key to maintaining the balance, we must be cautious in completing it.

12.3.9 雷厉风行 (adv, p)

Literal translation: Thunder-like resolveness and storm-like quickness.

Meaning: To act/move quickly and resolutely.

> 希望你们雷厉风行地执行统帅部的指令。
>
> [We] hope you can act quickly and resolutely to carry out the commands from headquarters.

12.3.10 冷嘲热讽 (adj, p, v)

Literal translation and meaning: Icy ridicule and burning sarcasm.

> 教师对学生的缺点不应冷嘲热讽。
> A teacher should not pour icy ridicule and burning sarcasm on his/her students.

12.3.11 灵丹妙药 (n)

Literal translation: Miracle drug and magical medicine, panacea.
Meaning: Something with a miraculous effect.

> 他认为减少政府干预乃是解决经济困难的灵丹妙药。
> He believes that the reduction of government intervention is a panacea for resolving the economic difficulty.

12.3.12 略胜一筹 (c, p, v)

Literal translation: A notch above.
Meaning: Slightly superior.

> 无论在思想深度上还是在技巧上，这部作品都略胜一筹。
> Both in the depth of its ideas and in its artistic execution, this work is a notch above that one.

12.3.13 落花流水 (adj, after "得")

Literal translation: Fallen flowers are carried away by running water.
Meaning: Utterly routed.

> 我军将来犯之敌打得落花流水。
> Our army utterly routed the invaders.

12.3.14 目中无人 (adj, p, v)

Literal translation: No one is within one's field of vision.
Meaning: To consider everyone beneath one's notice.

> 他刚刚出版了一本长篇小说就目中无人了。
> No sooner had he published his first novel than he considered everyone beneath him.

12.3.15 骑虎难下 (adj, v)

Literal translation: It is difficult to get off when riding on a tiger's back.
Meaning: Have no way to back down when something has been started.

> 货币改革开始以后，政府感到骑虎难下。
> The government feels it has no way of backing down after it initiated the monetary reform.

12.3.16 旗鼓相当 (adj, c, p, v)

Literal translation: In a battle, the banners and drums of the two sides are well-matched.
Meaning: Well-matched in competition.

> 辩论的双方旗鼓相当，很难预料谁会获胜。
> The two sides of the debate are well-matched, and it is difficult to predict who will win.

12.3.17 前车之鉴 (n)

Literal translation: The overturned cart ahead is a warning to the carts behind.
Meaning: A lesson drawn from the mistake made by others.

> 该国的前车之鉴值得所有发展中国家深思。
> The lessons of that country's unsuccessful development are worth noting by all developing countries.

12.3.18 千钧一发 (adj, c, p)

Literal translation: A ton of weight hanging by a hair.
Meaning: A very critical moment.

> 在这千钧一发的紧要关头，他挺身而出。
> In this extremely critical moment, he stepped forward bravely.

12.3.19 如获至宝 (p, v)

Literal translation and meaning: As if obtaining a treasure of the greatest value.

> 看到这本标价仅十元的旧书，王教授顿觉如获至宝。
> Finding this used book with a price tag of only 10 dollars, Professor Wang suddenly felt as if he had obtained a priceless treasure.

12.3.20 拾人牙慧 (p, v)

Literal translation: Pick the wit from another's teeth.

Meaning: Repeat what others have already said.

> 他的所谓新理论只是拾人牙慧而已。
> His so-called new theory is just a rehash of what others have said.

12.3.21 石沉大海 (c, p, v)

Literal translation: A dropped stone sinks to the bottom of the sea.

Meaning: Disappear forever.

> 报告递交以后，好像石沉大海，没有回音。
> After the report was handed in, there was never any response — as if a stone had been dropped into the sea.

12.3.22 束之高阁 (v)

Literal translation: Pack up something and put it into the attic.

Meaning: Brush something aside.

> 这个号称坚定的马克思主义者的人，在担任国家领导之后，很快就把马克思主义理论束之高阁。
> After being appointed the leader of the country, this so-called steadfast Marxist quickly brushed aside Marxism.

12.3.23 束手无策 (adj, v)

Literal translation: Fold one's hands helplessly and be unable to work out a plan.

Meaning: Be at loss for what to do.

> 新政府在严重的经济危机面前束手无策。
> Facing a serious economic crisis, the new government is at loss as for what to do.

12.3.24 双管齐下 (adj, v)

Literal translation: The right and left hands, each holding a brush pen, write different characters simultaneously.

Meaning: Do two things at the same time.

在他看来，经济改革和政治改革应当双管齐下。
According to him, economic reform and political reform should be carried out simultaneously.

12.3.25　水深火热 (adj, n)

Literal translation: Deep water and scorching fire.

Meaning: An abyss of suffering.

> 南京大屠杀以后，幸存者生活在水深火热之中。
> After the Nanjing massacre, the survivors lived in an abyss of suffering.

12.3.26　死灰复燃 (v)

Literal translation: Dying embers glowing again.

Meaning: Some previously put off (bad) force/practice revives.

> 要警惕不正之风死灰复燃。
> We should be vigilant so that the old unhealthy tendencies don't flare again.

12.3.27　螳臂当 (挡) 车 (adj, p)

Literal translation: A mantis tries to stop a chariot with its forelegs.

Meaning: Attempt to hold back an overwhelmingly superior force.

> "左派"反对改革的举动无异于螳臂当车。
> The Leftists' objection to the reform is no different from a mantis trying to stop a chariot.

12.3.28　体无完肤 (adj, after "得")

Literal translation: No part of the body remains intact.

Meaning: Be thoroughly refuted.

> 他将这种新理论批得体无完肤。
> He has thoroughly refuted this new theory.

12.3.29　天壤之别 (n)

Literal translation: A difference as great as the space between heaven and earth.

Meaning: Great difference.

中国人们的生活在改革前后有天壤之别。

The difference in the standard of living in China before and after reform is like night and day.

12.3.30 天衣无缝 (adj, c, p)

Literal translation: Divinely-made cloth is seamless.
Meaning: Flawless.

他的天衣无缝的回答使陪审团相信他是无辜的。

His flawless retort made the jury believe that he was innocent.

12.3.31 铁案如山 (adj, c, p, v)

Literal translation: The evidence is as strong as steel and is like an immovable mountain.
Meaning: Borne out by ironclad evidence.

他的罪行铁案如山。

His guilt is borne out by ironclad evidence.

12.3.32 同流合污 (adj, v)

Literal translation: To identify oneself with those of low conduct and to adapt oneself to a dirty social environment.
Meaning: Associate with evil elements.

我们绝不同恐怖主义组织同流合污。

We will never wallow in the mire with terrorists.

12.3.33 同舟共济 (p, v)

Literal translation: Cross a river in the same boat.
Meaning: Share the same destiny and help each other.

半个世纪以来，我们两个国家一直同舟共济。

For over half a century, our two countries have been helping each other — like crossing a river in the same boat.

12.3.34 土崩瓦解 (p, v)

Literal translation: Disintegrate as a piece of earth and fall apart as a piece of clay.

Meaning: Collapse/disintegrate thoroughly and quickly.

> 这道号称铜墙铁壁的防线在一昼夜间土崩瓦解。
> This line of defense which has long been considered impregnable fell apart in 24 hours.

12.3.35 玩火自焚 (adj, p, v)

Literal translation: To burn oneself to death by playing with fire.
Meaning: To make a foolish move that leads to self-destruction.

> 该地方政府在并无民意支持的情况下宣布独立，这无异于玩火自焚。
> That local government declared independence without popular support. It is no different than burning oneself to death by playing with fire.

12.3.36 万无一失 (c, p)

Literal translation: Do something ten thousand times without a single failure.
Meaning: Success is guaranteed.

> 由他来领导这项工程万无一失。
> His leadership over this project will guarantee its success.

12.3.37 望尘莫及 (p, v)

Literal translation: One cannot catch up with someone running ahead of him and can only see the dust he has left.
Meaning: Something is so superior that others cannot compare with it.

> 庄子将哲学同文学巧妙地结合在一起。在这一点上，其他哲学家望尘莫及。
> Zhuang Zi used vivid imagery to express his philosophical ideas. In this respect, other thinkers could not catch up with him and were left trailing far behind.

12.3.38 无孔不入 (adv, c, p)

Literal translation: Penetrate into every hole.
Meaning: Seize all opportunities.

> 在现代社会中，广告几乎无孔不入。
> In modern society, advertisements try to seize all opportunities to attract consumers.

12.3.39 小题大作 (adj, adv, p, c, v)

Literal translation: Compose a long article about a trivial topic.
Meaning: Make a fuss over a trifling matter.

> 政府将以全民公决的方式来决定是否修建收费公厕，这岂非小题大做？
> The government is going to decide whether to build paid public restrooms by means of national referendum. Isn't this much ado about nothing?

12.3.40 形形色色 (adj)

Literal translation: Various shapes and colors.
Meaning: All kinds.

> 记者要接触形形色色的采访对象。
> A reporter should have all kinds of interviewees.

12.3.41 喧宾夺主 (adj, c, p)

Literal translation: A presumptuous guest usurps the host's role.
Meaning: The secondary supersedes the primary.

> 这位旁听者的即席发言长达三十分钟，大有喧宾夺主之嫌。
> This uninvited speaker gave a 30-minute impromptu speech, making people resent his presumptuousness.

12.3.42 摇摇欲坠 (adj, c, p)

Literal translation: Something hanging above is shaky and is going to fall down.
Meaning: On the verge of collapse.

> 这位国王的残暴统治摇摇欲坠。
> The king's cruel regime is on the verge of collapse.

12.3.43 一唱一和 (adv, p, v)

Literal translation: One sings and the other joins in.
Meaning: Two parties advocate something in deliberate cooperation.

> 这两个国家一唱一和，宣扬所谓的国际新秩序。
> These two countries are singing a duet in their advocacy of the so-called "new international order."

12.3.44 异军突起 (p, v)

Literal translation: An unknown army makes a sudden appearance.
Meaning: A new force suddenly coming to the fore.

> 中国队异军突起，取得了世界冠军。
> As a new force suddenly coming to the fore, the Chinese team won the world championship.

12.3.45 易如反掌 (adj, c, p)

Literal translation: As easy as turning one's palm over.
Meaning: Very easy.

> 对他说来，将此文章译为中文易如反掌。
> For him, to translate this article into Chinese is a snap.

12.3.46 因噎废食 (adj, p, v)

Literal translation: Give up eating for fear of choking.
Meaning: To abandon something indispensable due to a rare accident/side-effect.

> 大规模基本建设势必带来交通问题，但我们绝不能因噎废食。
> Building large-scale infrastructure will of course bring about traffic problems, but we should not abandon it, just like we should not give up eating for fear of choking.

12.3.47 引狼入室 (adj, p, v)

Literal translation: To invite a wolf to one's own room.
Meaning: Open the door to a dangerous foe.

> 向这个有野心的企业家请求援助，无异于引狼入室。
> To seek help from this ambitious entrepreneur is no different from inviting a wolf to one's own room.

12.3.48 蒸蒸日上 (adj, adv, c, p)

Literal translation: Make daily progress like steam rising up.
Meaning: Thriving.

> 改革以后，中国的经济蒸蒸日上。
> Ever since reforms were introduced, the Chinese economy has been thriving.

12.3.49 指桑骂槐 (adv, p, v)

Literal translation: Point at the mulberry and scold the locust.

Meaning: Make an oblique accusation.

> 这位作家指桑骂槐地攻击党和政府。
>
> This writer is making veiled accusation against the party and the government.

12.3.50 众矢之的 (n)

Literal translation: The target of all arrows.

Meaning: Target of public criticism.

> 在这次会议上，主体性理论成为众矢之的。
>
> In this meeting, the theory of subjectivity became the target of everyone's attack.

12.4 结构性成语 (Structural Idioms)

结构性成语只是把表示一定意思的四个字习惯性地放在一起。

The structural idioms are those whose meanings can be understood directly by the characters that comprise them.

12.4.1 爱莫能助 (p, v)

To have sympathy but be unable to help.

> 对于你们的困境，我们爱莫能助。
>
> We have sympathy for your difficulties but we cannot help you.

12.4.2 半信半疑 (c, v)

Half-believe, half-doubt.

> 我对他说的话半信半疑。
>
> His speech made me half-believe and half-doubt.

12.4.3 不自量力 (adv, p, v)

Overestimate one's strength.

这个小国不自量力，竟然向超级大国发起进攻。
Overestimating its own strength, this small country dared to attack that superpower.

12.4.4 大同小异 (adj, c)

Basically identical with only minor differences.

两书的内容大同小异。
The contents of these two books are basically the same with only minor differences.

12.4.5 得不偿失 (adj, c, p)

Gains cannot offset losses.

我觉得大学生用过多时间打工赚钱得不偿失。
I think the pros don't outweigh the cons for a college student to spend a lot of time at a part-time job in order to make some money.

12.4.6 断章取义 (adj, p, v)

Distort the original meaning by incomplete quotation.

为了证明这位古代思想家的看法同当代科学一致，有些学者不惜对其著作断章取义。
In order to prove that this ancient thinker's ideas correspond with the principles of modern science, some scholars have gone so far as to distort the original meaning by partial quotation.

12.4.7 多此一举 (adj, c, p, v)

Unnecessary action.

他认为新施行的学生出入宿舍登记制度纯属多此一举。
He believes that the newly established student dorm registration rule is totally unnecessary.

12.4.8 奋发图强 (adv, v)

Work hard for prosperity (often of a country).

中国人民正在奋发图强，建设自己的国家。
The Chinese people are working hard for the prosperity of their country.

12.4.9 好逸恶劳 (adj, c, v)

Be fond of leisure and detest hard working.

> 此人从小好逸恶劳。
> This person has been eager to play and loath to work since he was a child.

12.4.10 化为乌有 (v)

Come to naught.

> 这场大火使他经营二十馀年的公司化为乌有。
> This fire totally destroyed the company he had managed for over 20 years.

12.4.11 患得患失 (adj, v)

Worry about personal gains or losses.

> 患得患失的人不能成为成功的政治家。
> A man who always worries about personal gains or losses cannot be a successful statesman.

12.4.12 恍然大悟 (v)

Suddenly see the light (understand).

> 听了他的话以后，我恍然大悟。
> Hearing what he said, I suddenly saw the light.

12.4.13 祸国殃民 (adj, v)

Bring calamity to the country and the people.

> 祸国殃民的四人帮把中国经济拖向崩溃的边缘。
> Calamity makers, the Gang of Four brought the Chinese economy to the verge of total collapse.

12.4.14 集思广益 (v)

Pool the wisdom of the masses.

> 只要集思广益，就可以解决这个棘手的问题。

This tough problem can be resolved by pooling the wisdom of the masses.

12.4.15 家喻户晓 (adj, v)

Known to all.

> 要使这项新政策家喻户晓。
> We should make this new policy known to all.

12.4.16 皆大欢喜 (v)

All sides are happy.

> 选举结果揭晓后，执政党和在野党皆大欢喜。
> The outcome of the election pleased both the ruling party and the opposition party.

12.4.17 结党营私 (v)

Form a clique to pursue selfish interests.

> 四人帮结党营私，给国家造成了重大的损失。
> The Gang of Four formed a clique to pursue their own selfish interests, bringing great losses to the country.

12.4.18 谨小慎微 (v, adj, adv)

To be cautious even about the smallest matters; overcautious.

> 他是一个谨小慎微的人。
> He is a man who is cautious even about the smallest matters.

12.4.19 尽善尽美 (adj, adv, n)

Perfection.

> 在创作上，这位作家总是追求尽善尽美。
> This writer always pursues perfection in his literary creation.

12.4.20 进退两难 (adj, p, v)

Difficult either to advance or to retreat; in a dilemma.

面对经济改革带来的社会动荡，政府感到进退两难。
Facing the social instability resulting from economic reform, the government feels unable to either advance or retreat.

12.4.21 惊心动魄 (adj, c, p)

Soul-stirring.

经过一场惊心动魄的搏斗，消防队员终于救出了被困在二楼的三名工人。
Through a soul-stirring struggle, the fire fighters finally saved the lives of the three workers who had been trapped on the second floor.

12.4.22 精打细算 (adj, p, v)

Careful calculation.

虽然他处处精打细算，还是未能避免公司的破产。
In spite of his careful calculation, he failed to prevent the company from going bankrupt.

12.4.23 利令智昏 (p, v)

Profit seeking makes one lose his intelligence.

总经理的野心招致公司宣告倒闭，这真是利令智昏。
The CEO's ambition led to the demise of the corporation, a good example of profit-seeking interfering with sound judgment.

12.4.24 流芳百世 (v)

Leave a reputation that will be appreciated by hundreds of generations.

他的英名将流芳百世。
He will leave a reputation which will go down to posterity.

12.4.25 流离失所 (v)

Be forced to leave home and wonder about.

日本侵略者使数千万中国人民流离失所。
Japanese invaders forced millions of Chinese to leave home and wander about.

12.4.26 屡教不改 (adj, v)

Refuse to mend one's ways despite repeated admonition.

> 对于屡教不改者一定要严加惩处。
> Heavy punishments should be administered to those who refuse to mend their ways despite repeated admonition.

12.4.27 美中不足 (adj, n)

A flaw in an otherwise perfect thing.

> 此种新型中文电脑软件使用方便，价格低廉，美中不足之处是某些字体不够美观。
> This newly developed Chinese software is easy to use and very affordable. Its only flaw is that some of its fonts are not very attractive.

12.4.28 民不聊生 (iph)

The people have no means of making a living.

> 在他的残暴统治下，民不聊生，怨声载道。
> Under his brutal reign, the people had no means of earning their livelihood and complaints were heard everywhere.

12.4.29 名不副实 (adj, c)

Be unworthy of the name or title.

> 称他为小说家名不副实，因为他只作文艺批评，从未创作过一本小说。
> He is unworthy of the title of novelist, because he only writes criticism and has never written a novel himself.

12.4.30 明哲保身 (adj, p, v)

Be worldly wise and play safe.

> 这位政治家明哲保身的态度使他在六十年的政治生涯中永远立于不败之地。
> This statesman's attitude of being savvy and playing it safe has kept him from being defeated in his 60-year political career.

12.4.31 莫名其妙 (adj, adv, p)

Cannot follow the subtle nuances (of a speech or an action); be baffled.

> 大多数听众对于他的演讲感到莫名其妙。
> Most of the audience fell baffled by his lecture.

12.4.32 内忧外患 (n)

Domestic troubles and foreign invasions or threats.

> 他刚刚当选总统之时，国家面临内忧外患。
> When he was elected president, the country was facing both domestic troubles and foreign threats.

12.4.33 宁缺毋滥 (adj)

Rather go without than have many unqualified.

> 该校在招生时一直本着宁缺勿滥的原则。
> When enrolling students, the principle of this school has always been that it is better to go without than to admit the unqualified.

12.4.34 弄巧成拙 (adv, p, v)

Try to be clever only to end up blundering; outsmart oneself.

> 政府弄巧成拙，其刺激经济增长的措施反而使股票市场出现前所未有的暴跌局面。
> The government's bold attempt to stimulate economic growth backfired, initiating an unprecedented fall in the stock market.

12.4.35 潜移默化 (adj, c, p)

Imperceptible influence and silent transformation.

> 老师的行为对学生有潜移默化的影响。
> The behavior of a teacher has an imperceptible influence on his/her students.

12.4.36 轻举妄动 (v)

Act without due consideration.

在这种微妙的时刻不应该轻举妄动。

Do not act rashly during this subtle moment.

12.4.37 穷凶极恶 (adj, adv, p)

Extremely ferocious and vicious.

穷凶极恶的德国法西斯将一千一百万人投入集中营，其中六百万系犹太人。

Extremely ferocious and vicious, German fascists imprisoned over 11 million people in concentration camps, 6 million of whom were Jewish.

12.4.38 忍无可忍 (adj, p, v)

The limit of one's endurance has been reached though one tries to endure.

我军在忍无可忍的情况下，被迫自卫反击。

At the end of our endurance, our army had to wage a counter-attack as a mean of self-defense.

12.4.39 日新月异 (adj, c, p)

Changing with each passing day.

北京的变化日新月异。

Beijing is changing with each passing day.

12.4.40 如临大敌 (adj, adv, v)

To act as if in front of a strong enemy; be extremely nervous.

对于这位宗教领袖的来访，当局如临大敌。

During the visit of this religious leader, the government was so nervous, as though walking on eggshells.

12.4.41 三思而行 (v)

Think again and again before making a move.

修改宪法可能导致大规模的抗议，很多人认为国会应三思而行。

To amend the constitution might cause large scaled protests, many people believe that the congress should think it over before making any move.

12.4.42 闪烁其词 (adj, adv, p, v)

Speak evasively.

> 这位发言人在回答问题时始终闪烁其辞。
> This spokesman was always evasive in his replies.

12.4.43 善始善终 (adv, p, v)

Start well and end well.

> 总理责成有关部门善始善终地处理好事故遗留下来的问题。
> The premier instructed the departments concerned to start well and end well in dealing with the problems left by the accident.

12.4.44 深恶痛绝 (p, v)

Have the most intense hatred for.

> 中国人民对帝国主义深恶痛绝。
> Chinese people hate imperialism bitterly.

12.4.45 神机妙算 (n)

Awesome strategy and shrewd calculation; foresight.

> 我们不能不佩服他的神机妙算。
> We have to appreciate his wonderful foresight.

12.4.46 实事求是 (adj, adv, p, v)

Look to the facts to find the truth.

> 希望你们实事求是地解决这个问题。
> [I] hope you can solve this problem in an objective and realistic way.

12.4.47 事半功倍 (adj, c)

Get twice the result with half the effort.

> 让农民自己修筑道路，可以取得事半功倍的效果。

Letting the peasants construct the road for themselves will mean getting twice the benefit at half the cost.

12.4.48 事与愿违 (iph)

The outcome is just the opposite to one's wish or expectation.

> 我们曾经希望能以和平方式解决两国的争端，但是事与愿违，对方的一再挑衅迫使我们使用武力。
>
> We had hoped to resolve the conflict between the two countries peacefully, but inspite of our hopes, the other country's repeated provocations forced us to take military action.

12.4.49 适可而止 (v)

Stop before going too far.

> 对年轻人的批评应该适可而止，不然就会伤害他们的积极性。
>
> If you criticize youngsters, you should stop before going too far. Otherwise it will harm their enthusiasm.

12.4.50 似是而非 (adj, adv, c)

Seemingly correct but actually wrong; plausible.

> 他的理论似是而非。
>
> His seemingly correct theory is actually wrong.

12.4.51 肆无忌惮 (adv, p)

(Do evil) unrestrainedly and unscrupulously.

> 由于有超级大国的支持，这个小国肆无忌惮地向邻国进攻。
>
> Backed by the superpowers, this small country attacked its neighbors unscrupulously.

12.4.52 随心所欲 (adj, adv, p)

Follow one's inclination; arbitrary.

> 我方无法接受你们如此随心所欲地解释双边条约。
>
> Our side cannot accept such an arbitrary interpretation of the bilateral agreement by your side.

12.4.53 贪生怕死 (adj, p)

Cravenly cling to life instead of braving death.

> 这个所谓的英雄实乃贪生怕死之辈。
> This so-called hero is in fact a man who cravenly clings to life instead of braving death.

12.4.54 听之任之 (adj, v)

Do nothing when something harmful is found.

> 对这种无理要求不能听之任之。
> We cannot simply condone such irrational demands.

12.4.55 同心同德 (adv, v)

Be of one heart and one mind.

> 我们两党应当同心同德地建设国家。
> We two parties should be of one heart and one mind in reconstructing the country.

12.4.56 突如其来 (adj)

Come all of a sudden.

> 这位作家在突如其来的赞誉面前保持了清醒的头脑。
> When fame came all of a sudden, this author retained a cool head.

12.4.57 徒劳无功 (adj, c, p)

Make futile effort.

> 总统的非洲之行徒劳无功。
> The president's visit to Africa was nearly a total waste of effort.

12.4.58 玩物丧志 (p, v)

Sap one's will to make progress by becoming engrossed in a hobby.

> 青年人不应该玩物丧志。
> A young man should not become so distracted by his bobbies that he loses his ambition.

12.4.59　危言耸听　(adj, adv, v)

Exaggerate things to scare people.

> 请不要危言耸听。中国的军事力量在十年内还不足以威胁西方。
> Please do not exaggerate things just to scare people. For the next 10 years, the military force of China will still be unable to threaten the Western world.

12.4.60　微不足道　(adj, c)

Too small to be worth mentioning.

> 我的贡献微不足道。
> My contribution is not worth mentioning.

12.4.61　唯利是图　(adj, p, v)

Be bent solely on profit.

> 在这位作者看来，唯利是图者现在越来越多。
> According to this author's view, there are more and more people who are bent solely on profit.

12.4.62　文不对题　(iph, v)

A composition is irrelevant to its theme.

> 我们都觉得她的讲话文不对题。
> We all felt her speech was totally off track and didn't address the subject at all.

12.4.63　文过饰非　(adj, adv, p)

Gloss over one's faults.

> 出了事故以后不可以文过饰非。
> When an accident happens, one should not gloss over it.

12.4.64　无法无天　(adj, adv, c)

Defy both civil and natural law.

该校某些学生无法无天，公然带枪来上课。

Defying both civil and natural law, some students of that school openly took guns with them to school.

12.4.65 无济于事 (v)

Of no avail.

经济形势如此严峻，仅靠发行债券已经无济于事。

Under such a severe economic situation, to issue bonds is of no avail.

12.4.66 无可奈何 (adv, c)

Have nothing to do to stop an action; have no alternative.

对于学生们的游行，政府无可奈何。

The government has no means of stopping the student demonstration.

12.4.67 无能为力 (adv, v)

Helpless.

医学界对于这种肾脏病仍然无能为力。

Doctors are still helpless when trying to treat this kind of kidney disease.

12.4.68 无懈可击 (adj, adv, c)

Unassailable.

他的发言无懈可击。

His speech is unassailable.

12.4.69 无中生有 (adj, adv)

Groundless(ly).

你们的指责完全是无中生有。

Your accusation is totally groundless.

12.4.70 先发制人 (adj, v)

Gain the initiative by striking first.

我军先发制人，在黎明前发起全面进攻。
Gaining the initiative by striking first, our army waged an all-out attack before dawn.

12.4.71 先入为主 (adj, v)

Be prejudiced by one's first impression.

请不要先入为主，多比较几种产品再作决定。
Please do not cling to your first impression and you should not make decision until you have compared a number of different products.

12.4.72 相形见绌 (c, v)

Pale by comparison.

在展销会上，这种牌子的产品大受欢迎，其他品牌相形见绌。
In the exhibition, the products of this brand were greatly welcomed whereas other brands paled by comparison.

12.4.73 想入非非 (v, adj)

Indulge in fantasy.

你应当采取现实主义的态度，切莫想入非非。
You should take a realistic attitude instead of indulging in fantasy.

12.4.74 兴高采烈 (adv, c)

In buoyant spirit.

中国人民正在兴高采烈地过春节。
Chinese people are celebrating New Year with a buoyant spirit.

12.4.75 循规蹈矩 (adj, adv, v)

Strictly observe the conventional rules and regulations.

如果循规蹈矩，这项工作在三年之内根本无法完成。
If we confirm strictly to convention, it will be absolutely impossible to finish this project in three years.

12.4.76 言不由衷 (c, p)

Speak insincerely.

> 我们知道她的话言不由衷。
> We know that she spoke insincerely.

12.4.77 言传身教 (n, v)

Teach by both verbal instructions and personal example.

> 他言传身教，培养出一批优秀的学生。
> Teaching by both verbal instructions and personal example, he has trained a number of excellent students.

12.4.78 言外之意 (n)

Meanings beyond the actual words; implication.

> 他的言外之意很清楚。
> Though not directly stated, the meaning behind his words is clear.

12.4.79 一举两得 (adj, c, p)

A single action brings about two (good) results.

> 山区种植果树既可以增加农民的收入，又可以减少水土流失，真可谓一举两得。
> To plant fruit trees in mountainous areas can not only heighten the incomes of the farmers there but also reduce soil erosion. It is really a single action that brings about two good results.

12.4.80 一丝不苟 (adv, p)

Not be the least bit careless.

> 他写作时总是一丝不苟。
> When writing, he is never the least bit negligent.

12.4.81 一无是处 (adj, after "得")

Devoid of any merit.

在她看来，这部电影一无是处。

According to her, this movie is devoid of any merit.

12.4.82 一厢情愿 (adv, p)

Wishful thinking of just one side (without reaction from the other side).

多年来，该国一厢情愿地追求和平，而对方却一再挑起战火。

For many years, that country has been seeking peace in a one side form of wishful thinking, while its adversary has initiated military conflicts again and again.

12.4.83 一意孤行 (adv, v)

Cling obstinately to one's [harmful] course.

当局一意孤行，使社会危机日益加深。

Because the government clings to its harmful policy, the social crisis is worsening day by day.

12.4.84 以身作则 (adv, v)

To play an exemplary role.

各级领导干部，都应该以身作则。

Leaders of all levels should play exemplary roles.

12.4.85 义正词严 (adv, c)

Stern words with the force of justice.

我国外长义正词严地驳斥了对方的诬蔑。

With the force of justice, our foreign minister sternly refuted his adversary's slander.

12.4.86 因陋就简 (adv, v)

Make do with whatever is available.

在农村发展普及教育应该因陋就简。

To develop elementary education in rural areas, it may be necessary to make do with whatever is available.

12.4.87 有条不紊 (adv, c)

All in good order without confusion.

> 财政制度的改革应当有条不紊地进行。
> The financial system should be reformed in an orderly fashion.

12.4.88 再接再厉 (adv, v)

Make persistent effort to build (upon one's present achievement).

> 望你们再接再厉，创造更好的成绩。
> [We] hope you make persistent effort to build upon your present achievements and accomplish even greater goals.

12.4.89 争先恐后 (adv)

Strive to be the first and fear to lag behind.

> 人们争先恐后地购买他的著作。
> People vie to be the first to buy his book.

12.4.90 志同道合 (c, p, v)

Cherish the same ideal and follow the same path.

> 这两位作家志同道合。
> The two writers cherished the same ideal and followed the same path.

12.4.91 置之度外 (v)

Give no thought to.

> 他早已将生死置之度外。
> For a long time he has given no thought to his own fate.

12.4.92 众望所归 (p)

Enjoy popular confidence.

> 由他来担任国家的最高领导是众望所归。
> Enjoying the confidence of the people, he was chosen to lead the country.

第十三章 · 新闻报导的规则和专门术语
Chapter 13 • News Reports: Rules and Special Expressions

13.1 消息来源 (Source of News)

常见的形式：机构 / 送稿人 (姓名) / 地点 / 时间 / 发稿或送稿方式

Normally, the source of news consists of the following elements: news agency/reporter or the person who reported the news/the place where the news came from/time/the way of sending the news.

13.1.1 机构 (agency)

常见的有通讯社或者报纸。

News agencies or newspapers are the most common ones.

> 本报巴黎15日电。
> This news was sent by telegram to our newspaper from Paris on the 15th.

> 新华社杭州8日电。
> This news was sent by Xinhua News Agency from Hangzhou on the 8th via fax.

13.1.2 送稿人 (person who sends the news)

常见的送稿人有：

The person who sends the news may be:

记者	reporter
特派记者 (特派员)	specially sent reporter
通讯员	correspondent
实习生	trainee

> 新华社重庆电(记者李诗)。
> This news was sent by Xinhua News Agency from Chongqing. (reporter: Li Shi)

> 本报东京特派员陈世昌八日电。
>
> This news was telegrammed by Chen Shichang, our newspaper's special correspondent in Tokyo, on the 8th.

13.1.3 时间 (time)

通常省略年/月，时间性特别强的消息还要加上小时。

Generally year and month are not mentioned. If the news is really new, important, and under development, hours may be added.

注意：消息来源中的日期常用廿 (二十) 和卅 (三十)。

Note: *Nian* (20) and *sa* (30) are sometimes used in news report.

> 中央社记者廿五日高雄电。
>
> This news was telegrammed by a reporter of the Central Agency on the 25th from Kao Hsiung.

13.1.4 地点 (place)

不常见的地点有时要加以说明。

If the place is not known to general readers, it should be explained concisely.

> 本报阿布扎比 (阿联酋) 11月15日电。
>
> This news was sent by our newspaper from Abu Dhabi (the United Arab Emirates) on November 15 via fax.

13.1.5 发稿或送稿方式 (ways of sending news)

常用的有：

The following are the most common ways:

电 = 电报或电传		telegram or fax
讯 = 消息		news (without mentioning the mean)
综合消息 = 综合各种消息来源		a synthesis of various sources

13.1.6 补充说明 (additional information)

在上述来源后还可加上补充说明。

The description of the source of the news can be followed by additional information.

> (中央社记者北京八日电) 大陆消息灵通人士今天说……

This news was sent by a reporter of the Central Agency from Beijing on the 8th via fax. Those in a well-informed circle of mainland China today said ....

13.1.7 新闻稿后的补充说明 (additional note in the end of a news report)

相关报导见第六版。
See page 6 for a detailed report.

讲话的全文另发，见第三版。
For the full speech, see page 3.

13.2 标题省略的规则 (Rules of Headlines)

13.2.1 在标题中常常省略量词 (measure words are often omitted in titles)

四歹徒抢劫银行
Four gangsters robbed a bank

五国外长会谈讨论中东局势
The five countries' foreign ministers discussed the Middle East crisis

13.2.2 标题中不用"了" (in headlines *le* is often omitted)

江泽民会见日本客人
Jiang Zemin met Japanese guests

13.3 新闻稿的语法和修辞特点 (Grammatical and Rhetorical Characteristics of the Text of News Reports)

13.3.1 "了"可以省略，但不是必须省略 (in many cases, *le* can, but not necessarily, be omitted)

法国卡车司机在全国高速公路近两百处设置（了）路障，数百个加油站被迫关闭（了）。此事件已在外汇市场上对法郎造成（了）打击。政府和司机代表昨天举行（了）第三轮会谈，但未能达成协议。
French truck drivers put up nearly 200 roadblocks. As a result, several hundred gas stations had to close. This incident has already affected the exchange rate of France.

The government and the representatives of the drivers yesterday held the third round of discussions, but no agreement was reached.

俄国总统前天在公民投票中赢得(了)压倒性赞成票，显示(了)人民对改革的支持。
The Russian president won decisively in the referendum, showing that the people support reform.

菲律宾总统为美国总统正式访菲举行(了)隆重的欢迎仪式。
The Philippines president hosted a grand ceremony to welcome the formal visit by the president of the United States.

13.3.2 其他省略 (other omissions)

俄国外(交部)长昨(乘坐)飞(机)抵(达)开罗，今(天)起将与埃(及)以(色列)两国外长讨论中东问题。
The Russian foreign minister arrived in Cairo by air yesterday, and will hold discussions with the Egyptian and the Israeli foreign ministers today.

13.3.3 新闻报导常用术语 (terms of news reports)

此间　　here

据悉　　It is said that …

获悉　　Got the information that …

透露　　disclose, reveal

披露　　disclose, reveal

13.3.4 国际关系新闻常用术语 (terms of international news)

会晤　　　meet

会见　　　meet (officials of the same level)

接见　　　meet (persons of lower level)

拜会　　　meet (persons of higher level)

谒见　　　visit (persons of superior)

一行　　　one's party

随行人员　accompanies, attaché

伉俪　　　husband and wife (honorific)

话别　　　talk with a guest who will leave soon

饯行	give a farewell dinner
临别	before parting
临行	before leaving
会谈	discussion
在座	be present
致函	write a letter to
照会	(A government) delivers a note to the government of another country
备忘录	memorandum
白皮书	white paper/book
声明	statement
最后通牒	ultimatum
最惠国	the most-favored-nations
中立国	neutral state
行径	(bad) behavior
指控	accuse, charge
率先	initiatively
挑起	start (a conflict)
事端	incident
挑衅	provoke
争端	conflict
离任	leaving one's position
到任	(a diplomat) arrives his/her post
国书	credentials
公海	high seas
主权	sovereign rights
领土	territory
领空	territorial air space
领海	territorial waters

大使	ambassador
公使	envoy, minister
参赞	counsellor
临时代办	chargé d'affaires ad interim
领事	consul
单方面	unilateral
双边	bilateral
多边	multi-lateral
霸权主义	hegemonism
沙文主义	chauvinism
陛下	His (Her, Your) Majesty
阁下	His (Her, Your) Excellency
殿下	His (Her, Your) Royal Highness
邦交	to establish diplomatic relation

13.3.5 政治新闻常用术语 (terms of political news)

与会	participate in a meeting
出席	attend a meeting
列席	participate in a meeting as informal attendant
政局	political situation
示威	demonstration
罢工	strike
暴动	rebellion
暴乱	riot
骚乱	turmoil
暴徒	gangsters, rebellions
政变	coup d'état
兵变	mutiny

组阁	form a cabinet
全民公决	plebiscite
民意测验	public opinion poll
弹劾	impeach
朝野	governing party and opposition
杯葛	boycott

13.4 报刊术语 (Terms of Newspapers and Periodicals)

晚报	evening newspaper
周报	weekly
半月刊	bi-weekly
月刊	monthly
双月刊	bi-monthly
季刊	quarterly
社论	editorial
评论员文章	commentor's article
编者按	editor's note
头版	front page
头条	lead (news) stories
版	page
通栏标题	banner headline
发行量	circulation

同美国的报纸比较，中国的报纸版面较少，但是中国的报纸常常有小说连载，这是美国报纸很少有的。中国的晚报比较发达，在一些大城市，晚报比日报更受欢迎。

In comparison with American newspapers, Chinese newspapers have less pages. However, there are often, if not always, fiction serials in newspapers, which are rare for American newspapers. In addition, China has many influential evening newspapers. In many big cities, evening newspapers do much better than day newspapers.

第 十 四 章 • 论 文
Chapter 14 • Academic Essays

读学术论文的主要困难有两个，一是结构复杂的长句较多，二是有些学者喜欢生造新词。这两点也正是同其他形式的书面语的主要区别。

To read an academic essay, the major difficulties are: First, there are many long sentences with complicated structure; second, some authors like to create new words. Actually, they are the two features that distinguish academic essays from other sub-styles of written language.

14.1 长句的结构与分解 (Structure of Long Sentences and Their Reduction)

在学术论文中，可以见到不少非常复杂的句子。这种句子通常是所谓"欧化"句。虽然很多批评家认为这种句子毫不可取，我们也不鼓励同学们模仿，但是有一些学者就是用这种风格来写文章，所以不能不加以研究。解读这种句子的关键是抓住其中心结构，把一个长句分解为几个短句。

In modern Chinese academic essays, one can find many very complicated long sentences. They are often so called "Europeanized" sentences. Although many critics believe that this style is worth nothing, and we do not encourage students to imitate, some scholars insist on writing such sentences. Thus, we should have some knowledge of this style. The key to understand this kind of sentences is to grasp the central structure, and to divide a long sentence into several parts.

> 在过去几年中，除了少数价格控制措施以外，妨碍国内货物流动的区域管理性壁垒和曾在八十年代盛行并引起重大问题的不利因素大部分均已消除。
> Except for some price control measures, most of the regional administrative barriers to domestic mobility of goods and the disadvantageous factors which prevailed and caused great problems in 1980s have been removed in the past couple of years.

中心结构：在过去几年中，大部分壁垒和不利因素已经消除。
分解：区域管理性壁垒妨碍国内货物的流通，还有一些不利因素曾在八十年代盛行，并引起重大问题。这些壁垒和问题在过去几年中大部分已经消除了，只有一些价格控制措施是例外。

对通货膨胀将居高不下的预期已经扼杀了促进花销猛涨和重现有生气的经济增长所需要的长期债券和有价证券的市场。

High, permanent inflation expectations have killed the long-term bond and equity markets that are required to fuel a spending boom and the regeneration of robust economic growth.

中心结构：对通货膨胀的预期扼杀了长期债券和证券市场。

分解：人们预期通货膨胀将居高不下，这样就扼杀了长期债券和债券的市场。而要促进花销增加，重现经济的生气，需要长期债券和债券市场。

成功的一个关键是认识到需要对团体观念给以更多的关注，并且承认我们对于毫无约束的自私自利和侵略性的自我中心论的容忍已经太过分了。

A key to success is to recognize the need for greater attention to the idea of community and to acknowledge the excesses of our toleration to unbridled self interest and aggressive egoism.

中心结构：我们需要关注团体观念，我们对自私自利和自我中心论的容忍太过分了。

分解：团体观念很重要，我们需要更多地关注这个观念；我们容忍自私自利和自我中心论，即使自私自利达到了毫无约束的程度，即使自我中心论是侵略性的，我们也能够容忍，这种态度太过分了。

对世界的精神性的认识帮助我们将人的宗教性作为使人生得到全方位发展的一条道路，而与此同时，对于作为万物尺度或者作为从不受挑战的主宰自然的天赋权威的人道的排斥一切的关注却把精神领域降格为毫不相干的东西，并且也把自然仅仅当作消费的对象。

While the recognition of the spirituality of the world helps us to appreciate human religiosity as a way of living the fullness of life in all its dimensions, the exclusive focus on humanity as measure of all things or as endowed with the unquestioned authority of dominion over nature relegates the spiritual realm to irrelevance and reduce nature to an object of consumption.

中心结构：对于人道的过分关注使我们轻视精神领域和自然。

分解：我们认识到世界有精神性。这种认识帮助我们把人的宗教性看成一条道路，在这条道路上，人生能够得到全方位的发展。但是与此同时，我们把人道看成万物的尺度，或者把人道看成从来不受挑战的主宰自然的天赋权威。对于这样一种人道的排斥一切的关注使我们轻视精神领域和自然。精神领域成了毫不相干的东西，自然只是消费的对象。

14.2　新词的生造 (Creation of New Words)

新词的生造有多种情况。比较有规律的是通过添加后缀来使动词或形容词转化为名词，或者将名词进一步抽象化。这种词性转化在欧洲语言中是很普通的，但是对于中文来说却是一种比较新的东西，可以说是欧化的另一个重要的表现。下面的一些词汇是转化的典型例子，大部分已经不是新词，使用已经相当广泛。对于新词可以类推。

There are various ways to create new words. What is relatively traceable is the conversion from verbs or adjectives to nouns, and from concrete nouns to abstract nouns by adding suffix. Such conversion is quite common in European languages but new in Chinese. This is probably another typical influence of Western languages on Chinese written expressions. The examples below are some typical conversions, and most of the words are already well accepted. For new conversions we can follow these examples to comprehend.

14.2.1 度 (degree)

除了表示程度的意义之外，还有改变词性的功能。放在动词或形容词之后，可以使之成为名词。

Apart from meaning degree, it may convert a verb or an adjective into a noun when added as a suffix to the verb or adjective.

深度	depth
广度	breadth
知名度	notability
透明度	openness

14.2.2 性 (nature)

除了表示性质的意义以外，还有改变词性的功能。如果放在动词或形容词之后，可以使之成为名词。也可以放在名词之后，使之成为更抽象的名词。

Apart from meaning "nature/property," it may convert a verb or an adjective into a noun when added as a suffix to the verb or adjective. It may also be added as a suffix to a noun to make it more abstract.

可能性	possibility
冒险性	adventurousness
先进性	progressiveness
象徵性	symbolization
欺骗性	deceptiveness

妥协性　　tendency towards compromise

积极性　　activeness

宗教性　　religiosity

14.2.3 化 (becoming)

"化"作为后缀，放在动词、名词或形容词的后面，形成一个动词或者名词，表示从一种状态或性质到另外一种状态或性质。

As a suffix added to a verb, noun, or an adjective to indicate the change from one nature/state to another nature/state.

革命化　　revolutionize/revolutionizing/revolutionized

现代化　　modernize/modernization/modernized

老龄化　　aging

美化　　　beautify

强化　　　strengthen

深化　　　deepen

14.3 借用科学名词 (Use Scientific Terms)

近年来的一个新的趋势是在人文科学和社会科学的学术论文中借用自然科学的词汇，特别是同计算机相关的词汇。下面是一些例子：

A new trend of recent years is to borrow new terms from the natural sciences, especially computer technology, for the writing of academic works in humanities and social sciences. Following are some examples:

一个企业要兴旺发达，不仅要注意硬件，也要抓好软件。
To be prosperous, an enterprise should not only pay attention to the "hardware" but also make great efforts to improve the "software."

"硬件"在这句话里是指企业的设备等等看得见的东西，"软件"是指职工的培训，领导与工人的关系等不容易看见的东西。

In this sentence, "hardware" indicates visible things such as equipment, and "software" indicates invisible elements such as the training of workers and the relationship between the management and the workers.

传统的干部选拔制度采用黑箱作业，不利于竞争和发现优秀人才。

The traditional system of cadres promotion is a "black-box" operation. It is not helpful for competition and search for talent.

这句话里的"黑箱作业"是指"不公开"的意思。

In this sentence, "black-box" means "not open to the public."

这个地区的领导阶层思想保守，经济发展也十分落后，缺乏深化改革的政治生态。

The leaders of this region are conservative, and the economic development there falls far behind. Thus, it falls short of the ideal political ecosystem for deepening reform.

这里的"生态"实际上是"环境"的意思。

In this sentence, "ecosystem" actually means "environment."

第十五章·文学描写
Chapter 15 • Literary Writings

文学作品的形式和内容极为丰富，很难一概而论。这里，仅介绍文学作品中常见的两种语言现象。

The styles and contents of literature are extremely abundant, and it is difficult to discuss every one of them. Here we deal with two aspects one will frequently encounter.

15.1 比喻 (Analogy)

文学作品常常使用比喻的手法，常见的比喻句型除了口语使用的"好像……""……似的"以外，还有下面一些比较特殊的句型。有关的词汇可以分为前置和后置两种，可以单独使用前置或后置，也可以一起使用。

Analogies are frequently used in literature. Besides "*haoxiang …*" and "*… side*" patterns, there are a number of other patterns as shown below. The related words can be classified into two groups: (1) those before an analogy, and (2) those after an analogy. The two groups of words can be used either independently or combined.

15.1.1 前置 (words placed before an analogy)

15.1.1.1 如……

他的书法如长江大河，豪迈奔放。
His calligraphy is bold and unrestrained, like a great river running forward.

15.1.1.2 有如……

在他看来，人生有如没有地图的旅行，达到目的也就意味着生命的终结。
To him, life is like a trip without a map. When one reaches a destination, his life comes to an end thereby.

15.1.1.3 犹如……

噩耗犹如一声惊雷，大家呆呆地站着，说不出话来。
This sad news was like striking thunder, and all the people were stupefied and could not say even a single word.

15.1.1.4 如同……

他知道在一个九百万人的大城市寻找一个既无地址又不知姓名的人如同海里捞针，但他还是抱着一线希望。
He knew in such a big city of over 9 million people, to find a person without an address and name is like recovering a needle from the haystack, but he still had a ray of hope.

15.1.1.5 好似……

一幅优秀的摄影作品，好似一瓶陈年美酒，令人回味无穷。
An excellent photograph is like a bottle of mellow wine of endless aftertaste.

15.1.1.6 恰如……

他的处境十分危险，恰如一叶小舟在狂风恶浪中穿行。
He is in a very dangerous situation, like a small boat going against giant waves.

15.1.1.7 恰似……

学习驾驶恰似学习游泳，经验远比书本重要。
To learn how to drive is just like learning swimming. Experience is more important than knowledge learned from books.

15.1.2 后置 (words placed after an analogy)

15.1.2.1 ……般

演唱在暴风雨般的掌声中结束。
The performance ended with thunderous applause.

15.1.2.2 ……一般

他觉得大都市的生活如同地狱一般。
He felt that life in the metropolis was as terrible as in hell.

15.2 四字格式 (Four-character Structure)

在文学作品中，特别是在散文和报告文学中，常用四字成语和类似四字成语的四字结构短语。短短的一篇文章常有数十个甚至上百个四字短语。此外，商品广告中也常用类似的结构。四字格式虽然简短，但是却可以包含比较丰富的内容。这种四字格式的用法和成语基本一致。

In literature, especially in prose and reportage, four-character idioms and idiom-like four-character phrases are abundantly used. A very short article may contain several dozen or even over a hundred such phrases. These kinds of phrases are also frequently used in advertisements. Four-character phrases are short in form but rich in contents. The rules for the four-character phrases are roughly the same as four-character idioms.

下面是一些常见的四字格式的类型：

The following are some common types of four-character phrases:

15.2.1 四个同类词的迭加 (comprising four words of the same nature)

江河湖海   big rivers, rivers, lakes, and seas

15.2.2 两个词性相同的双音节词的迭加 (comprising two two-character words of the same nature)

英勇顽强   courageous and unyielding

小心谨慎   careful and cautious

15.2.3 第一字和第三字分别修饰第二字和第四字 (the first and the third characters are respectively the modifiers of the second and the fourth characters)

巧笑佯羞   hypocritical laughter and artificial shyness

15.2.4 第一和第三字是话题，第二字和第四字分别是对第一和第三字的评论 (the first and the third characters are topics and the second and the fourth characters are respectively comments on them)

质次价高   quality is poor and price is high

15.2.5　前二字为话题，后二字为评论 (consist of a two-character topic first and a two-character comment to follow)

警戒森严　　security is tight

情趣高雅　　interest is graceful

15.2.6　前二字修饰后二字 (the first two characters modify the last two characters)

最佳药方　　the best remedy

密切合作　　close cooperation

15.2.7　前两字重复或后两字重复 (either the first or the last two characters repeat each other)

场场爆满　　all seats occupied in every show/game

样样精通　　excellent at every skill

困难重重　　multiple difficulties

金光闪闪　　glittering

15.2.8　半固定半开放结构 (semi-variable structure)

有些四字格式中的两个字是固定的，另外两个字可以更换。

For some four-character phrases, two characters are fixed and the others are variable.

15.2.8.1　一⋯⋯ 不⋯⋯

一言不发　　keep silent

一文不值　　worth nothing

15.2.8.2　⋯⋯中有⋯⋯

苦中有乐　　happiness in bitterness

喜中有忧　　worries in happiness

动中有静　　stillness in motion

15.2.8.3 互不……

互不侵犯　do not attack each other

互不干扰　do not disturb each other

第 十 六 章 • 广 告 和 产 品 说 明 书
Chapter 16 • Advertisements and Product Manuals

16.1 广告 (Advertisements)

广告有极为丰富的类型，很难详述。这里限于介绍广告中的一些常用词汇和短语。

There are many types of advertisements and it is difficult to deal with all of them. Here we will introduce words and phrases frequently seen in the advertisement texts.

16.1.1 产品或服务广告常用语 (words or phrases frequently used in product or service advertisements)

特价	special discount price
清仓大甩卖	inventory sale
半价	half price
买一送一	buy one get one free
优惠	discount
九折	10% off

为庆祝营业五周年，东方旅行社定于三月十五日起进行为期一周的特价销售活动。苏州一日游买一送一(周末除外)，新辟黄山三日游半价(优惠期间只发三班，请从速定购)，国内国际机票一律九折优惠。订票电话：868-8888。

To celebrate its fifth anniversary, the Oriental Travel Agency will have a special one-week promotion starting on March 15. For day trips to Suzhou, make your reservation for two for the price for one (exclude weekends). Enjoy a 50% discount for the new three-day tour to Mt. Huangshan (only three tours are offered during the promotion period, so book now), and 10% off for all international and domestic flight tickets. For reservations, please call 868-8888.

16.1.2 招聘广告常用语 (words or phrases used in job-opening advertisements)

诚聘	sincerely invite applications for a position

高薪聘请	invite applications for a high pay job
诚聘英才	invite high calibre applicants
待遇从优	job with great salary and benefits
机会均等	equal opportunity employer
有……经验者优先	those who have the experience of ... will be favorably considered

太平洋广告公司诚聘英才

太平洋广告公司是上海最大的中外合资广告公司之一，因扩大国际业务需要，现高薪招聘高级英文译员一名，限英语国家著名大学毕业，欢迎有一定中文水平的外籍人士应聘。

有志应聘者，请在一周内将个人简历、学位证明、身份证或护照影印件寄至上海南京路一号301室太平洋广告公司人事部。本公司将尽快安排合格人员面试。接到通知以前请勿来电话询问或来访。

Pacific Advertising Co. Invites High Calibre Applicants

The Pacific Advertising Co. of Shanghai is one of the largest joint ventures of this field. To meet the need of international expansion, we are seeking an English translator, and offering a highly competitive salary. The successful candidate should be a graduate of a prestigeous college of an English-speaking country. Foreign nationals with some command of the Chinese language are welcome to apply.

Applicants should send their résumés and photocopies of their academic certificates, and personal ids or passports within a week to:

Pacific Advertising Co.

Personnel Department

Suite 301

1 Nanjing Road, Shanghai

Interviews will be arranged for qualified applicants as soon as possible. Please do not call or visit in person before being notified.

16.3 产品说明书 (Product Manuals/Instructions)

感冒灵

本品为纯中药制剂，采用传统配方，用最新科学方法精制而成。

主要成分：桑叶、菊花等

主治：伤风感冒，头疼咳嗽

用法：一日三次，每次三片，饭后服用，小儿酌减

禁忌：服药期间禁油腻辛辣食品

　　　　肝肾功能不全者慎用

"Smart" Cold Medicine

This product is made purely from Chinese medicinal herbs based on a traditional prescription and refined with the most advanced scientific technique.

Main ingredients: mulberry leaves, chrysanthemum, and other herbs.

Indications: chiefly for colds, flus, headaches, and coughs.

Dosage: 3 pills each time; 3 times per day. Taken after meals. Children should reduce the dosage according to their ages.

Contradiction: Avoid having greasy and hot foods when taking this medicine. Patients with liver or kidney disease should be cautious.

第十七章·其他各类应用文
Chapter 17 • Other "Applied" Writings

17.1 警示语言（Warnings）

警示语的特点是文字特别简短。虽然涉及的内容多与日常生活密切相关，但是却倾向于使用和口语不同的词汇。

Conciseness characterizes the texts of warning signs. Although their contents are often closely related to everyday life, the tendency is to avoid using common words.

17.1.1 严禁（strictly prohibited）

本组语言中语气最强。

The strongest expression of this group.

> 严禁吸烟　No Smoking
>
> 严禁摄影　No Photography
>
> 严禁入内　Do Not Enter

17.1.2 禁止（prohibited）

比上一种说法略弱。

This expression is a little bit less stronger than the above one.

> 此处禁止钓鱼　Fishing is not allowed in this area
>
> 禁止鸣笛　　　No whistling

17.1.3 不得（may not, should not）

> 不得携包入内　　　Bags are not allowed in

| 不得中途退场 | No exit half way through |
| 不得携带易燃易爆物品 | Do not bring in inflammable or explosive materials |

17.1.4 请勿 (please do not ...)

请勿践踏草坪	Keep off the lawn
请勿喧哗	Do not make noise, please
请勿随地吐痰	No spitting
请勿乱扔果皮纸屑，违者罚款	Do not litter, violators are subject to fines
山石危险，请勿攀登	The rocks are slippery, no climbing
请勿与司机交谈	Do not talk to the driver

17.1.5 其他常见警示语 (some other frequently seen warnings)

游人止步	No visitors
商品售出，概不退换	All sales are final. No returns or refunds
谨防扒手	Watch thefts!

17.2 表格 (Forms)

来宾登记表 Visitor's Registration Form

姓名　Name
性别　Sex
工作单位　"Work Unit" (Employer)
来访时间　Date of Visit　　　年 year　　月 month　　日 date
由　from　　　　　　　　　　时 hour　　分 minute
至　through　　　　　　　　　时 hour　　分 minute
会见何部门何人　Whom to visit and that person's department
事由　Reason to visit
携带何物　Things to bring with
来访者签字　Signature of the visitor
被访者签字　Signature of the visited

出门时请将此表交还门卫。
Please fill in the form and return it to the door guard when leaving.

17.3 规则 (Rules and Regulations)

借书证 (Rules printed on a library card)

1. 本证限持证人使用，不得转让，离校时务必归还。

   This card is to be used by the cardholder and is not transferable. One must return it upon leaving school.

2. 凭此证可借阅普通图书十本，小说一本。

   With this card, one may borrow 10 general books and 1 work of fiction.

3. 借期两周，可续借两次。逾期不还者每天每本罚款五角。

   Loan period is two weeks and book(s) can be renewed twice. Borrowers who fail to return book(s) in time will be subject to a fine of 50 *fen* per item per day.

4. 期刊杂志与工具书不可携出馆外。

   Periodicals and reference books may not be charged out.

5. 阅览善本图书需先提出申请，说明阅览理由。

   To read rare books, please submit an application first to state the reason for reading such books.

6. 丢失图书必须赔偿相同版本新书一本，或缴纳原书价格三倍以上之罚金。

   Borrowers who lose a book must buy a new book of the same edition as redemption or pay a fine of at least three times the original price.

7. 爱护图书，请勿污损。

   Please take care of the books and do not damage them.

8. 短期生领取此证时需缴纳押金五百元。

   Short-term students must pay a deposit of 500 *yuan* before getting this card.

第十八章·信函
Chapter 18 • Correspondence

信函的形式有新旧之分。旧式信函属于文言文的范畴，不在本书讨论的范围之内。新式信函结构比较自由，同口语比较接近。然而，在新式信函中，特别是比较正式的信函，也常常采用一些旧式信函的套语，所以需要在此加以介绍。

Chinese letters can be divided into two styles: the traditional style and the contemporary style. Since the traditional style is really a form of classical Chinese, it is beyond the scope of this book. The contemporary style allows for more freedom in structure and is closer to spoken Chinese. However, when people write letters in contemporary style, especially relatively formal letters, they often adopt some of the fixed expressions used in traditional correspondence. Thus when we introduce the letters of the contemporary style, we need to examine some of the most frequently used traditional expressions.

18.1 一般信函 (Common Correspondence)

一般信函的结构可以分成以下几个部分:

A typical letter can be divided into the following parts:

18.1.1 收信人称谓以及附带敬语 (the recipient and the respectful words for the recipient)

对收信人最平常的称谓是姓名加先生/女士/同志或者加上其职称(与英文将职称放在名字前面不同)。受西方信函的影响，也可以在最前边用"亲爱的"。如果收信人是长辈或者职务较高，可以将"亲爱"换成"敬爱"、"尊敬"等。

The most common form of address is the name of the receipient plus Mr./Ms/Comrade or the recipient's position. (This is unlike English where the title comes before the name.) Western influence has led to the term, "*qin'aide*" or "dear," being used as a salution sometimes. If the recipient is of an elder generation or holds a high position, "dear" tends to be replaced by terms that mean "respectfully beloved" or "respectful."

亲爱的李中民同志：
Dear Comrade Li Zhongmin,

敬爱的刘梅校长：
Respectfully Beloved Principal Liu Mei,

旧式的传统称谓和敬语很多。需要注意的是，在很多情况下，为了表示对收信人的尊敬，不能直接称呼这个人，而只能称呼收信人所在的地方。另外，称谓中的"兄"和"弟"常常不是真的兄弟而是表示比较密切的朋友关系。下面列举的是一些在新式信函中还能常常见到的称谓和敬语。

There are many traditional addressings and related respectful words. It is worth notice that in many cases, in order to pay respect to the recipient, the sender should not address the recipient directly but use a place word instead. In addition, the words *xiong* (elder brother) and *di* (younger brother) are often used to indicate intimate relation between friends, not to mean real brothers. Below are some traditional forms of address and respectful words that can still be seen in contemporary letters.

大人   *Lit.*: great man/woman (used to address parents and senior relatives)

膝下   *Lit.*: under the knees [of the recipient] (used to address parents and grand parents)

尊前   *Lit.*: in front of your respectfulness (used to address relatives of elder generations)

尊右   *Lit.*: to the right of your respectfulness (usage is the same as 尊前)

慈鉴   *Lit.*: for your benevolent reading (usage is the same as 尊前)

帐下   *Lit.*: under the curtain of your teaching platform (used to address a teacher)

足下   *Lit.*: under your feet (used to address a friend of the same generation)

大鉴   *Lit.*: for your great reading (usage is the same as 足下)

雅鉴   *Lit.*: for your graceful reading (usage is the same as 足下)

如晤   *Lit.*: as though I were meeting you (used to address a younger friend)

下面是这些敬语的应用范例：

Below are some examples how these words are used:

双亲大人膝下
Dear Father and Mother,

舅父大人慈鉴
Dear Uncle,

谷方教授帐下
Dear Professor Gu Fang,

利民弟如晤

Dear Mr. Limin,

18.1.2 开端应酬语 (words before the main contents)

在开始信函的主要内容之前，一般需要有表示礼貌的应酬语。常见的有：

In general, some words to express courtesy are needed before starting the main body of a letter. Typical expressions include:

18.1.2.1 表示怀念 (to express that one misses the recipient)

久未通讯，怀念之至。

It has been a long time since our last correspondence, and I miss you very much.

一别三载，甚为怀念。

It has been three years since our last meeting, and I miss you very much.

18.1.2.2 表示收到对方的来信 (to express "your letter was received")

惠书敬悉

Lit.: Your letter, which was a favor to me, was carefully read with respect.

前接来函

Lit.: Your letter was received the day before yesterday.

承赐华翰

Lit.: I received the excellent letter you presented.

展阅云笺

Lit.: I unfolded and read your letter which seems to come down from Heaven.

18.1.2.3 表示知道有关对方的消息 (to express "I heard")

恭悉   *Lit.*: with reverence, I heard

敬悉   *Lit.*: with respect, I heard

敬闻   *Lit.*: with respect, I heard

近闻   *Lit.*: recently I heard

欣闻   *Lit.*: I was glad to hear that

惊悉   *Lit.*: it surprised me to hear that (a bad news) / I am sorry to hear that

18.1.2.4 对回信不及时表示歉意 (to apologize for being late to reply)

近日公务繁忙，未能及时回信，十分抱歉。

I have been busy at work recently, so I could not reply earlier, and I am very sorry for this.

18.1.3 正文 (main contents)

没有固定格式，语言应当简洁，有礼貌。

There is no fixed format. The language should be concise and polite.

18.1.4 结尾应酬语 (respectful words placed after main contents)

在信函的主要内容之后，一般应该有格式比较固定的表示礼貌的应酬语，主要有下面一些内容:

In general, after the end of the main body of the letter, there should be some fixed courteous expressions. Typical expressions include:

18.1.4.1 表示这封信不能完全表达我的心意 (to mention that this letter cannot fully express my feelings and ideas)

不尽所怀
I cannot fully express what I thought.

纸短情长
The paper sheet is too short to express my long-lasting affection to you.

言不尽意
Language cannot fully express one's ideas.

18.1.4.2 希望收信人原谅自己写得太潦草 (hope the recipient will pardon the sender for writing in a rush)

幸恕草草
It would be my fortune if you would pardon me for writing in such a rush.

18.1.4.3 希望收信人回信 (to express hope that the recipient will respond to the letter)

如蒙不弃，乞赐兰言。
Lit.: Should you not give me up, I would beg you to grant me your valuable words.
Meaning: I hope I will have the honor of hearing back from you.

18.1.4.4 希望收信人保重 (hope the recipient will care for his/her health)

春寒料峭，尚乞自珍。
Lit.: The early spring is still very cold, please allow me to beg you to take care of yourself.

18.1.5 函末祝颂语（wishes that end the letter）

18.1.5.1 对父母或其他长辈（to parents or others of elder generation）

祝您健康长寿
Lit.: I wish you good health and longevity.

敬请金安
Lit.: I respectfully wish you golden peace and harmony.

敬颂大安
Lit.: Respectfully I wish you great peace and harmony.

18.1.5.2 对朋友（to friends）

最简单和常见的祝词是"祝好"，"祝万事如意"或"祝合家平安"。也可以根据对方的职业或者根据写信的时节来决定祝颂语。

The most common wishes are *zhuhao* (best wishes), *zhu wanshi ruyi* (I hope everything goes well with you) or *hejia ping'an* (wish your whole family safety and peace). Wishes may also be made according to the profession of the recipient or the season/holiday.

顺颂撰祺（对作家）
Lit.: I wish you happy writing. (used for an author)

恭祝暑安（在夏天用）
Lit.: Wish you a peaceful summer. (used in summer)

祝新年快乐
Wish you a happy new year.

18.1.6 署名（signature）

中文信函署名一般分为下面一些部分：（一）写信人同收信人的相对关系；（二）姓名（关系较近时常省略姓）；（三）书写方式（也是由同收信人的关系决定）；（四）写信人所在地（一般只是旅行在外时才使用）；（五）日期。

In general, the signature of a Chinese letter includes the following contents: first, a mention of the relationship between the sender and the recipient; second, name of the sender (if the sender and recipient have a close relationship, the surname is often omitted); third, the "way" of writing (selected according to the relationship between sender and recipient); fourth, the current place of the sender (not mentioned if the sender is at home); and fifth, date.

儿东民敬上
99年12月18日

Your son Dongmin writing in respect on the 18th day of December, 1999

弟仲基拜启
五月六日

Lit.: Your younger brother Zhongji writing in great respect to you the recipient on the 6th day of May

"弟"常常并不意味着写信人真的比收信人年轻。有时一个称"弟"的写信的人实际上会比收信人稍稍年长，这只是为表示对收信人尊敬的一种客气的自称方式。

Note: *di* in many cases does not mean a real younger. Actually the sender may be even slightly older than the recipient. This is only a courteous way to show respect to the recipient.

愚兄鹏远手书于沪

Lit.: Your stupid elder brother Pengyuan handwriting from Shanghai

当写信的人明显地年长于收信人的时候，"愚兄"是一种客气的自称方式。

Note: "Stupid elder brother" is a courteous form of self-address when the sender is senior to the recipient.

18.1.7 附言 (P.S.)

一般用"又及"来引导。

In general, it is written after *youji*.

18.1.8 一般信函的例子 (an example of a common letter)

林安教授雅鉴：

久未通讯，甚为怀念。上周收到您托陈茹女士带来的信函及所附新作，喜出望外。本应及早回复，无奈教务繁忙，望能见谅。

大作已拜读。您对先秦道家思想的来源的分析十分新颖和精辟。上古医学的确影响了道家思想的发展。然而，在我看来，儒家的思想似乎也与医家有关。例如，儒家的中庸哲学同医家的阴阳平衡之说有很多相同之处。此点不应忽略。

我将出席今秋在长沙举办的中国古代思想讨论会，想您也会参加，希望届时能有机会详谈。

言不尽意，幸恕草草。顺颂

夏安

云峰手书
1999年8月7日

Lit. translation:

To Professor Lin An's graceful reading,

It has been long since our last correspondence, and I miss you very much. Last week I received your letter as well as your new book you asked Ms. Chen Ru to bring to me. I was surprised and pleased. I should have replied to you earlier; unfortunately, I have been too busy with teaching and I wish you would pardon my lateness.

I have already read your great new book. Your analysis of the sources of the Pre-Qin Daoism is both original and accurate. The ancient medicine of China indeed exerted great influence on the development of Daoism. To my knowledge, however, Confucianism is also related to Chinese medicine. For instance, the Confucian philosophy of the "Golden Mean," and the theory of keeping yin and yang in balance taught by Chinese medicine have great similarities. It seems that this relation should not be ignored.

I will take part in the Conference on Ancient Chinese Thought in Changsha this fall, and I believe you will be present, too. At that time, we should have an opportunity to enjoy a long and thorough discussion.

My words cannot fully express my ideas and I will feel fortunate if you might pardon me for writing in such a rush.

Wish you a nice summer.

Yunfeng Handwriting on August 7, 1998.

18.2 申请书与履历表 (Letter of Application and Résumé)

中文的申请书与英文的习惯差别不大，但所附履历表的形式则有不同，通常是由远及近，与英文相反。

The style of Chinese application letters is similar to English style. However, the résumé attached to it is somehow different. Both education and working experience are listed in chronological order, unlike in English where they are listed in reverse order.

> 首都师范大学中文系：
>
> 　　近悉贵系将于今年暑假举办高级汉语进修班，本人非常感兴趣，特此申请参加。我从1993年开始学习汉语。1994年在哈佛大学完成初级汉语课程以后，曾到台湾师范大学学习汉语半年。1996–97年在耶鲁大学读研究生期间，继续学习高级汉语和古代汉语课程。现在能够熟练地阅读中文报刊和短文。但是我希望有更好的会话和写作能力。
>
> 　　随信寄上我的履历和我的中文老师的推荐信。希望能将有关表格及邀请信尽快寄给我。以便办理签证等手续。
>
> 　　谢谢。
>
>
>
> 吴其人
>
> 1998年9月8日
>
>

Lit. translation:

Department of Chinese Language of Capital Normal University:

Recently I have learned that your esteemed institution will be holding a summer program for advanced Chinese learners. I am very interested in this program and would like to apply to join it.

I started to learn Chinese in 1993. After completing beginners' Chinese at Harvard University in 1994, I went to Taiwan Normal University to learn Chinese for half a year. During my postgraduate study in Yale University in 1996–97, I continued taking advanced Chinese courses and ancient Chinese courses. Now I have a good command of written Chinese and am able to understand Chinese newspapers and essays, but I wish to have a better ability in conversation and composition.

Enclosed please find my résumé and a letter of recommendation from my Chinese teacher. I hope that you will send me an invitation letter and related forms at your earliest convenience so that I can start visa application and other formalities.

Thank you.

Wu Qiren
September 8, 1998

简历
Résumé

姓名：吴其人
Name: Wu, Qiren

性别：女
Sex: Female

年龄：35
Age: 35

学历：
Education:
    1990–1994
        在哈佛大学学习，1994年获得人类学学士学位。
        Harvard University. Obtained B.A. in Anthropology.
    1994–1995
        在台湾师范大学国语中心学习汉语并获得证书。
        Mandarin Center, Taiwan Normal University. Studied Chinese and was awarded certificate of study.
    1996–1997
        在耶鲁大学历史系攻读中国历史专业研究生。
        Yale University. Studied Chinese History in History Department.

工作经验：

Work Experience:

    1992–1994

        在哈佛大学博物馆整理中国古代文献（半工半读）。

        Harvard University Museum. Part-time research assistant on ancient Chinese documents.

    1994–1995

        在台湾师范大学教英语写作（半工半读）。

        Taiwan Normal University. Part-time English composition teacher.

主要著作：

Published Works:

    "对楚文化的人类学研究"，发表于《古代中国》杂志1993年第10期。

    "An Anthropological Approach to Chu Culture," in *The Early China*, Issue 10 (1993).

    "清代中央政府同地方政府的关系"，发表于李克教授主编的《中国的现代转化》一书，1996年耶鲁大学出版社出版。

    "The Relationship between the Central Government and the Local Governments during the Qing Dynasty," in *The Modern Transition of China*, edited by Professor Rick (Yale University Press, 1996).

语言：

Languages:

    英文（母语）English (mother language)

    中文（中级水平）Chinese (intermediate level)

18.3　推荐信 (Letter of Recommendation)

中文推荐信与英文推荐信的区别不大，但一般写推荐信的人不详细说明自己的身分和地位。

Chinese letters of recommendation are similar to English ones. However, the author will not detail his/her own position and status.

北京师范大学对外汉语教学中心负责同志：

    兹推荐我的学生吴其人女士前往贵中心进修汉语。吴女士是耶鲁大学历史系研究生，她的研究课题是中国近代外交史。为了能够熟练阅读有关中文文献，她选修了我开设的"高级汉语"课程。她的听、说、读、写能力在全班都属于上等水平，但给我留下更深印象的是她的刻苦努力和对于中国文化的了解的全面性。如果贵中心能接受吴女士的申请，本人将不胜感激。如果需要对她的汉语水平作进一步的了解，请通过下述电话号码与我联系：(512)668–3990。

朱文华

1998年9月5日

Lit. translation:

To the authority of Chinese Language Teaching Center for Foreigners, Beijing Normal University:

I write to recommend my student Ms. Wu Qiren to pursue advanced study in Chinese at your esteemed center. Ms. Wu is now a graduate student at the Department of History, Yale University, and her subject of research is the diplomatic history of modern China. In order to read Chinese materials related to her research, she took my course in advanced Chinese. She excelled in all aspects: listening comprehension, speaking, reading, and writing. However, what impressed me the most was her diligence as well as her comprehensive understanding of Chinese culture. I would be grateful if you would accept her to study at your center. In case you need further information about her qualification in Chinese language, please do not hesitate to contact me at the telephone number below: (512) 668–3990.

Zhu Wenhua
September 5, 1998

18.4 请柬 (Invitation)

请柬的特色是文字简洁，目的以及时间地点清楚，最后的套语是"敬请莅临"。注意：中国人的请柬一般不要求被请人答复是否出席。

An invitation should be succinct with clear mentioning of the purpose, time, address. The idiomatic ending sentence is "you are respectfully invited to come." In general, a Chinese invitation will not request the invitees to reply whether they will come.

> 龙年春节即将到来，为感谢您对我社工作的大力支持，现定于2月1日下午五时在红星电影院举行新春作者联欢会，会后放映电影《我的故乡》，敬请莅临。
> The Year of the Dragon is coming. In order to express our thanks to you for your generous support to our society, a New Year celebration party with authors will be held on February 1 at 5 p.m. at Red Star Cinema. There will be a show of movie "My Hometown" afterwards. You are respectfully invited to come.

练习
Exercise

一. 填空 (Fill in the blanks with proper words)

1. 在人权问题上，东方国家（　　　　）西方国家的看法不完全一致。
2. 政府必须有效地控制环境污染，（　　　　）将有可能对整个地区的生态产生不可逆转的损害。
3. 中国总理的演讲幽默（　　　　）富有感染力。
4. 发达国家的儿童往往面临营养过剩的问题，（　　　　）发展中国家的儿童（　　　　）常常营养不良。
5. 修建铁路可将西部的矿产更为方便地运往沿海地区，（　　　　）可刺激沿线地区的经济发展。
6. （　　　　）能提出若干例证，本文的说服力将会更强。
7. 我们（　　　　）降低发展速度，也不能接受这种条件苛刻的贷款。
8. 诚然，日本的经济近年来不太景气，但这（　　　　）不意味着该国已经不再是一个经济强国。
9. 这项提案（　　　　）美国的反对（　　　　）未能通过。
10. 美日外长（　　　　）农产品问题举行会谈。
11. 只有深入地研究孔子所处时代的社会环境，才能对（　　　　）思想有正确的理解。
12. 市场上销售的（　　　　）些"新药"其实只是原来的药物加上新的包装。
13. 总理的美国（　　　　）行极为成功。
14. 他（　　　　）说的和我（　　　　）看到的有很大的差距。
15. 新总统认为政府机构（　　　　）庞大，表示要在任期内消减三千名工作人员。
16. 政治家们大都主张民主，（　　　　）何为民主，则有很多不同的见解。
17. 这本题为《中国思想史》的著作竟然没有提到孔子，（　　　　）怪事？
18. 将这位青年作家同鲁迅相提并论（　　　　）免太过分了。

二. 多选填空 (Multiple choice)

1. 他曾任（　　）跨国公司驻香港代表。
   A. 其　　B. 某　　C. 为

2. (   ) 得到美国等西方国家的援助，该国也很难实现经济复兴。
   A. 若   B. 之所以   C. 即便

3. (   ) 大量进口石油，不如投资开发本国的油田。
   A. 如果   B. 岂可   C. 与其   D. 宁可

4. 发展重工业 (   ) 是重要的，但是农业的重要性也不应当忽视。
   A. 固然   B. 虽然   C. 与其   D. 岂非

5. 这部电影 (   ) 受到国内外观众的喜爱是由于它反映了人民的愿望。
   A. 虽然   B. 然则   C. 如若   D. 之所以

6. (   ) 对方毫无诚意，我政府决定无限期中止谈判。
   A. 尽管   B. 鉴于   C. 因而   D. 假如

7. 该小说作者原 (   ) 北京钢铁公司工人，所以十分熟悉工人的生活。
   A. 乃   B. 为   C. 非

8. 这家新开业的饭店 (   ) 供三千人同时用餐。
   A. 可   B. 能   C. 当

9. 该公司的经理 (   ) 对这起事故负主要的责任。
   A. 应   B. 可   C. 由

10. 登记结婚时，男女双方均 (   ) 持本人有效证件。
    A. 可   B. 须   C. 能

11. 这本 (   ) 大众喜爱的小说在几小时内销售一空。
    A. 把   B. 被   C. 为

12. 不解决通货膨胀问题，(   ) 经济发展的其他问题都将无法解决。
    A. 因此   B. 则   C. 故

13. 美国不应 (   ) 中国视为敌人。
    A. 同   B. 与   C. 将

14. 国有企业改革目前 (   ) 最困难的阶段。
    A. 处于   B. 在于   C. 忙于

15. 因暴风雪的影响，昨天本市共发生重大交通事故二十余 (   )。
    A. 起   B. 个   C. 件

16. 美国不断对别国的政治进行批评，(   ) 是要让各国效法美国的制度。
    A. 不无   B. 从未   C. 无非

17. (   ) 将中国人口控制在十三亿以下是新政府面临的主要问题。
    A. 如何   B. 是否   C. 与否

18. 此事关系到国家发展的方向，(   ) 不经讨论就作出决定？
    A. 是否   B. 能否   C. 岂可

19. 国会正在讨论 (   ) 提前举行大选。
    A. 尚未   B. 是否   C. 何曾

20. 获得国际大奖的电影 (   ) 必受到国内观众的喜爱。
    A. 不   B. 何   C. 未

21. 面对突然发生的金融危机，政府（　　）准备。

    A. 毫不   B. 不必   C. 毫无

22. 我们不放弃使用武力（　　）好战，而是要维护国家的统一。

    A. 并非   B. 并无   C. 无从

三. 翻译 (Translation, from Chinese to English)

1. 京沪万人集会庆祝抗日战争胜利五十周年。

2. 全国作协昨选出新任主席和秘书长。

3. 关于道家思想的发展细节，请参阅拙著《道家源流考》。

4. 十八岁以下青少年不得观看本片。

5. 此处不得吸烟，违者罚款五元。

6. 他将自己仅有的二百元钱寄往灾区。

7. 他因贩卖毒品被处以极刑。

8. 同这个危险的国家进行军事合作无异于引火烧身。

9. 老年居民最担心的莫过于医疗保险问题。

10. 时下，足球是中国最热门的运动。

11. 第十五届全国人民代表大会将于近日召开。

12. 接到通知后，请速来办公室与王主任联系。

13. 中国一向主张，国家无论大小，一律平等。

14. 他屡次提出辞职，而公司则一再挽留。

15. 这个城市的污染问题迄今尚无明显改善。

16. 席间，宾主频频举杯，共祝两国友谊万古常青。

17. 临行前，他专程拜访了大学时期的老师。

18. 春节前夕，到处洋溢着浓厚的节日气息。

19. 大选在即，两党候选人纷纷到这个人口最多的地区拉票。

20. 学生学习期间不得工作的规定现已废除。

21. 继研制成功太阳能汽车之后，该研究所又开发了太阳能汽艇等新产品。

22. 著名诗人高原昨日凌晨在京逝世，享年九十一岁。

23. 主席和副主席均未参加这次会议。

24. 他对美国大选的结果颇为关心。

25. 他断然否定曾在会议上发表过这种言论。

26. 中国的人口占世界的五分之一强。

27. 虽然遇到了世界性经济危机，这个国家的出口只下降了两个百分点。

28. 中国大城市收入超过三万元的居民已超过两成。

29. 近年来，来此旅游的人数以每年百分之十以上的速度递增。

30. 毋庸置疑，两国的合作将对世界和平作出积极贡献。

四. 用下列成语完成句子 (Complete version B of the sentences with the idioms given below)

邯郸学步	班门弄斧	杞人忧天	四面楚歌	胸有成竹	天衣无缝
画蛇添足	滥竽充数	同流合污	爱莫能助	旗鼓相当	家喻户晓
坐收渔利	拔苗助长	一鸣惊人	拾人牙慧	略胜一筹	言不由衷
日新月异	双管齐下	束手无策	死灰复燃	三思而行	万无一失
天壤之别	易如反掌	目中无人	一无是处	宁缺毋滥	小题大做

1. A. 他的回答没有任何漏洞。
   B. 他的回答（　　　　　　）。

2. A. 你是著名作家，我只是初学者，我不想在你面前乱说一通。
   B. 我不想（　　　　　　）。

3. A. 这件事本来不重要，他却坚持要在讨论后投票决定。
   B. 他这样做真是（　　　　　　）。

4. A. 他作翻译作了二十多年，让他翻译这篇文章太容易了。
   B. 翻译这篇文章对他来说（　　　　　　）。

5. A. 这位候选人对当选十分有信心。
   B. 这位候选人（　　　　　　）。

6. A. 这篇论文写得不错，但最后一章漏洞很多，还不如不要。
   B. 这篇论文的最后一章在我看来是（　　　　　　）。

7. A. 这位演员本来唱歌唱得不错，但是她偏偏要模仿一位台湾歌星的风格，结果她的欣赏者越来越少。
   B. 这位演员做的事情无异于（　　　　　　）。

8. A. 参加这次讨论会的很多人对要讨论的问题根本没有研究。
   B. 很多与会者不过是（　　　　　　）。

9. A. 这种看法早有人提出过，但是他却拿过来当成自己的新发现。
   B. 他所谓的新发现不过是（　　　　　　）。

10. A. 有人认为用电脑会降低人的智力，我觉得这种担心没有必要。
    B. 认为电脑使人脑退化的担心是（　　　　　　）。

11. A. 这个演员演的第一个电影就获得了国际大奖。
    B. 这个演员（　　　　　　），首部电影就获得国际大奖。

12. A. 你是艺术家，不应该和那些商人一起干坏事。
    B. 艺术家不应与奸商（　　　　　　）。

13. A. 这两支球队的实力差不多，很难预料谁会获胜。
    B. 两支球队（　　　　　　）。

14. A. 由于这两个候选人互相攻击，把对方的丑闻揭露出来，结果双双落选。一个
      本来没有希望的候选人当选了。

    B. 两个候选人互揭丑闻使第三个候选人（   ）。

15. A. 这张画各方面都比那一张好一些。

    B. 这张画同那张画比，（   ）。

16. A. 由于发表了一系列错误言论，这位总经理的反对者越来越多。

    B. 这位总经理已处于（   ）之境地。

17. A. 这个城市的发展速度很快，每天都有新的变化。

    B. 这个城市的变化（   ）。

18. A. 新中国成立不久，吸毒的现象就消失了。但是最近几年，又有人开始吸毒
      了。

    B. 吸毒的现象在中国（   ）。

19. A. 这个人很骄傲，谁也看不起。

    B. 这个人实在是（   ）。

20. A. 他觉得这本书没有任何值得看的地方。

    B. 在他看来，此书（   ）。

21. A. 我同情你的困难，很想帮助你，但是却没有办法。

    B. 对于你的困难，我实在是（   ）。

22. A. 这个国家的东部非常发达，但是西部却非常落后。

    B. 该国的东部与西部有（   ）。

23. A. 这种政策政府宣传了很长时间，家家都知道了。

    B. 这种政策已经（   ）。

24. A. 我们宁可少招几个学生，也不能降低录取标准。

    B. 本校的招生政策是（   ）。

25. A. 他认为工业和商业都很重要，应该同时发展。

    B. 他认为发展工业和商业应该（   ）。

26. A. 金融危机来得这么突然，政府一点办法也没有。

    B. 政府在金融危机面前（   ）。

27. A. 这是关系到你的前途的事，我觉得你应该好好想想再作决定。

    B. 你应该（   ）。

28. A. 她说这些不是真心话。

    B. 她（   ）。

29. A. 父亲希望儿子有出息，每天让儿子读书读到半夜，结果儿子的学习成绩反而
      下降了。

    B. （   ）对孩子没有好处。

30. A. 他很细心，让他做这件事绝对不会出差错。

    B. 让他做这件事（   ）。

五. 阅读理解 (Reading comprehension)

一. 国际新闻 (International news)

新华社纽约8日讯

出席联合国代表大会的我国代表团团长日前在此间会见南非外长后对记者说，中国一向重视同包括南非在内的非洲国家的合作与交流，他透露，中国主席和南非总统将于明年实现互访。南非外长将于下周赴北京进行为期三天的工作访问，以确定两国元首互访的具体日程安排。

1. The head of the Chinese delegation to UN assembly
   A. is going to meet the foreign minister of South Africa.
   B. met the foreign minister of South Africa the day before yesterday.
   C. met the foreign minister of South Africa recently.
2. China
   A. has been paying attention to its relationships with African countries.
   B. will pay greater attention to its relationships with African countries.
   C. needs help from South Africa to cooperate with other African countries.
3. The South Africa foreign minister will
   A. accompany South African president to visit Beijing next week.
   B. meet the Chinese president in Beijing next week.
   C. detail the next year's head of state visits between the two countries.

二. 经济新闻 (Economic news)

新华社北京消息

根据国家统计局今天公布的数字，我国去年农作物再次获得创记录丰收，其中棉花产量比上年增长近三成，油料和其他经济作物也获得较大幅度的增长。全国农民的人均收入已突破两千元，人均拥有住房面积达11.5平方米。国家统计局的有关人士指出，我国农村经济发展的速度仍呈现较明显的地区差别，沿海地区已提前进入小康，而西部一些山区尚未摆脱贫困。

1. Last year, China's cotton crop increased by nearly
   A. 3%.
   B. 30%.
   C. three times.
2. Last year, the average annual income of Chinese peasants
   A. was over 2,000 yuan.
   B. increased 2,000 yuan as compared with the previous year.
   C. increased by 11.5%.

3. The rural development of China is not in balance because

  A. overpopulation is taking over farm land in coastal areas.

  B. the mountainous areas in western China are still very poor.

  C. peasants in some areas are beyond the control of the government.

三. 社会新闻 (Social news)

一辆载有危险品的卡车昨日凌晨在福州至厦门的高速公路上突然起火燃烧，经消防队员和附近驻军的奋力抢救，已将烈火扑灭，一度中断的高速公路在事故发生四小时后恢复正常。事故的原因以及对于周围农田可能造成的污染正在调查之中。据目击者称，事故中多人因吸入化学烟雾受伤，但无人死亡。

1. The accident occurred in

  A. the early morning.

  B. the rush hours.

  C. a summer morning.

2. The highway between Fuzhou and Xiamen

  A. reamined open in spite of the accident.

  B. was shut down for hours after the accident.

  C. has been shut down until the pollution evaluation is over.

3. Several people were injured because of

  A. inhaling chemical smoke.

  B. the crash during the accident.

  C. an explosion.

四. 论文 (Treatise)

以往的中国历史研究多强调中国文化的静态性与稳定性，这同研究者本身的教育背景和专业训练不无关系。换言之，以政治、经济、哲学为中国历史发展主线的学者倾向于发现中国历史中的恒定结构，忽视艺术、民俗等方面的不断变异的特徵。

1. According the author,

  A. stability witnessed in Chinese history is caused by the Chinese education system.

  B. Chinese culture has both stable and dynamic elements.

  C. economic structure is the key to understanding Chinese politics, philosophy and arts.

2. The analysis implies that

  A. a historian should have a wider range of knowledge.

  B. arts and folklore played a great role in history than common recognition.

  C. Both A and B.

亚洲金融危机不仅冲击了许多亚洲国家的政治和经济秩序，也在意识形态方面对若干年来甚为流行的东亚模式提出了尖锐的挑战，不少西方学者以为此次危机标志着对于西方自由资本主义模式的普世性的再肯定，因而消除残存的东方色彩是克服危机的唯一选择。然而，一些东方学者却援引大中国文化圈（大陆、台湾、香港、新加坡）遭受冲击较小的事实说明儒家的伦理仍然具有优越性。

3. Some Western scholars believe that
    A. the Asian financial crisis is caused by mal-administration of the governments.
    B. the Asian financial crisis has challenged the East Asia Model.
    C. the Asian financial crisis will not come to an end till Western countries pro-vide enough aid.
4. Some Eastern scholars believe that
    A. Confucianism is the root of the financial crisis.
    B. Confucianism may have alleviated the shocks of the crisis.
    C. Confucianism has proven to have superb ethics during the crisis.

五．启事 (Job opening)

南海出版集团公司招聘启事

南海出版集团公司是中国发展最快的中港合资出版公司之一，公司总部位于风景秀丽的海南省海口市。因业务需要，现高薪招聘高级英文编审一名，负责本公司大型项目——英文本《中国文化百科全书》的编审顾问工作。

应聘人限英语为母语者，持有英语国家著名大学文科专业硕士以上学位，对中国文化有比较全面的了解，并能流利地听说汉语，有在出版社工作经验者将优先考虑。

经本公司录用后，除提供高薪外，还将在任期内提供高级住房一套以及全套医疗保险。此职位任期约三年，自2000年9月1日始。

有志应聘者，请在一周内将个人详细简历、学位证明、著作或论文样本、身份证或护照影印件寄至海南省海口市滨海路一号301室南海公司人事部。本公司将尽快安排合格人员面试。

1. The major task for this position is
    A. to translate Chinese texts into English.
    B. to write an encyclopedia about Chinese culture in English.
    C. to supervise and advise the edition of an encyclopedia in English.
2. The successful candidate should be
    A. Non-Chinese citizen with command of the Chinese language.
    B. born and educated in an English-speaking country.
    C. an experienced editor knows both English and Chinese.

3. Besides salary, the holder of this job will enjoy

    A. free housing.

    B. health insurance.

    C. both A and B.

六. 产品说明 (Product manual)

健美减肥茶

  本品以优质绿茶，加入多种名贵中草药，用最新科学方法精制而成。经常饮用可以助您消除体内多馀脂肪，使您身体更加健美，精力更加充沛。对高血压、糖尿病等与肥胖有关的疾病有一定的辅助疗效。

  饮用方法：将茶叶袋放入杯中，加热开水后约等五分钟，即可饮用。每日饮用两到三杯，不宜过量。饮用本品期间，请勿服用其他减肥药物。

1. The main ingredient of this product is:

    A. green tea.

    B. medicinal herbs.

    C. vitamins.

2. According to the text, this product

    A. surely has curative effect on obesity related diseases.

    B. may be helpful to curing some obesity related diseases.

    C. makes you slim by stimulate your desire for physical exercise.

3. One is suggested to drink the tea

    A. two or three cups a day.

    B. as much as possible.

    C. together with other fat-fighting medicine.

七. 规则 (Regulations)

宿舍守则

1. 所有住宿学生应遵守此守则，建设具有社会主义精神文明的学生宿舍。
2. 本宿舍仅供本校学生使用，严禁校外人员留宿。
3. 本宿舍为男生宿舍，来访女生限于在一楼会客室接待，不得进入其他楼层。
4. 楼道内不得堆放任何私人物品，违者罚款。
5. 节约能源，离开宿舍时请随手关灯。
6. 注意防火，请勿在宿舍内使用电炉及其他大功率电器。
7. 提高警惕，遇有可疑人员请立刻通知门卫。
8. 保持宿舍清洁卫生，不得乱扔废弃物品。
9. 晚十一时以后，不得在宿舍内播放音乐或大声交谈。

1. Since this dormitory is for male students only, female students
    A. are not allowed to enter the building at all.
    B. must register before entering the building.
    C. can only stay in the reception hall of the first floor.
2. In the dormitory, residents are not allowed to use
    A. one's own desk lamp.
    B. electric fan and air conditioner.
    C. microwave oven.
3. Who will be fined according to the rules?
    A. One who has left the light on.
    B. One who has placed an empty bookshelf in the hallway.
    C. One who was loud after 11:00 p.m.

六. 写作 (Composition)

中国文化大学今年暑假将举办一个中国文化讨论会。这个讨论会没有邀请外国学者参加。你是美国哈佛大学的博士研究生，研究中国历史，请你写一封申请信，表示你非常想参加这个讨论会，并附你的简历。

答案 (Answers)

一. 填空 (Fill in the blanks with proper words)

1. 同，与 or 和
2. 否则，不然 or 如若不然
3. 而
4. 而……则……
5. 且，并 or 并且
6. 若 or 如
7. 宁愿
8. 并
9. 因……而……
10. 就
11. 其
12. 某
13. 之
14. 所……所……

15. 过于
16. 至于
17. 岂非
18. 未

二. 多选填空 (Multiple choice)

1. B
2. C
3. C
4. A
5. D
6. B
7. B
8. A
9. A
10. B
11. C
12. B
13. C
14. A
15. A
16. C
17. A
18. C
19. B
20. C
21. C
22. A

三. 翻译 (Translation, from Chinese to English)

1. Over ten thousand people gathered respectively in Beijing and Shanghai in commemoration of the 50th anniversary of the victory of Anti-Japanese War.
2. A new chairperson and a new secretary of National Authors Association were elected yesterday.
3. For the details of the development of Taoist thought, please refer to my *Textual Research in the Sources of Taoism*.
4. People under the age of 18 may not watch this movie.

5. Smoking is not allowed here. Violators will be subject to a fine of five dollars.

6. He mailed 200 dollars — that was all he had — to the disaster area.

7. He was sentenced to death for drug trafficking.

8. To engage in military cooperation with this dangerous country is not unlike drawing fire against oneself.

9. The biggest concern for senior citizens is the health care.

10. Nowadays soccer is the most popular sport in China.

11. The 15th Session of the People's Congress of China will be held in a few days.

12. Contact Mr. Wang, the office director, as soon as you get this notice.

13. China has been insisting that all the countries, big or small, should be equally treated.

14. He delivered resignation report for several times, but the company management urged him to stay once again.

15. No evident improvement has been made so far to the pollution issue of this city.

16. During the banquet, hosts and guests toasted frequently, wishing the friendship between the two countries would last forever.

17. Before he left, he made a special visit to his college professor.

18. In the eve of Chinese New Year, the holiday atmosphere can be found any-where.

19. The upcoming general election drives the candidates from both parties to come to this most populated region to canvass votes.

20. The rule that a student may not work during the school term has been abol-ished.

21. This institute developed solar motor boats and other new products after it had succeeded in developing a solar car.

22. Gao Yuan, a famous poet, passed away in the early morning of yesterday at the age of 91.

23. Neither the chair nor the vice chair attended this meeting.

24. He has great concern about the result of the general election of the United States.

25. He completely denied that he had made this kind of speech in the meeting.

26. The population of China is over one fifth of the world population.

27. Despite world-wide economic crisis, the export of this country decreased only by 2%.

28. In big cities of China, there are over 20% of residents whose annual income surpass 30,000 *yuan*.

29. In recent years, visitors to this place have increased 10% each year.

30. Beyond doubt, the cooperation between the two countries will be a positive contribution to the world peace.

四. 用下列成语完成句子 (Complete version B of the sentences with the idioms given below)

1. 天衣无缝
2. 班门弄斧
3. 小题大做
4. 易如反掌
5. 胸有成竹
6. 画蛇添足
7. 邯郸学步
8. 滥竽充数
9. 拾人牙慧
10. 杞人忧天
11. 一鸣惊人
12. 同流合污
13. 旗鼓相当
14. 坐收渔利
15. 略胜一筹
16. 四面楚歌
17. 日新月异
18. 死灰复燃
19. 目中无人
20. 一无是处
21. 爱莫能助
22. 天壤之别
23. 家喻户晓
24. 宁缺毋滥
25. 双管齐下
26. 束手无策
27. 三思而行
28. 言不由衷
29. 拔苗助长
30. 万无一失

五. 阅读理解 (Reading comprehension)

一.
1. C
2. A

3. C

二.

1. B
2. A
3. B

三.

1. A
2. B
3. A

四.

1. B
2. A
3. B
4. B

五.

1. C
2. B
3. C

六.

1. A
2. B
3. A

七.

1. C
2. C
3. B